What Readers and Critics say about the Poetry of Felix Dennis

'Felix Dennis is the real thing. I love reading his verse and you will, too.'
— Stephen Fry, *actor, writer and director*

'The uncrowned Poet Laureate… he writes in the language of the soul.'
— Christopher Rush, *author*

'His poetry sings like a summer breeze through the fairground.'
— Sir Paul McCartney, *musician and songwriter*

'He is the very essence of English poetry — lyrical, rhythmic, emotional.'
— Jon Snow, *television newscaster*

'I love his poetry. With moments of real genius, some of his poems will last as long as poetry is read.'
— Benjamin Zephaniah, *poet*

'If Waugh were alive, he would fall on Dennis's verse with a glad cry of recognition and approval.'
— John Walsh, *The Independent*

'I enjoy his poetry immensely.'
— Mick Jagger, *singer and songwriter*

'An engaging monster, filled with contradictions and reeking of sulphur.'
— *The Times*

'He invokes sorrow as fast as regret, pain as readily as passion, love as tenderly as murderous rage.'
— Shirley Conran, OBE, *author*

'The best poet writing in the English language.'
— Tom Wolfe, *critic and author*

'The most satisfying collection of poetry I have ever read.'
— Tracy Farnsworth, *editor, roundtablereviews.com*

'Beautifully crafted, accessible and unforgettable. To watch him perform is pure magic.'
— Clare Fitzsimmons, *Stratford Observer*

'At least one of these poems will be instantly anthologised.'
— Melvyn Bragg, *broadcaster and author*

'Total, utter joy… so real, so readable and so enjoyable.'
— Richard Fair, *bbc.co.uk*

'Talent at once wise and maddeningly childish, optimistic and grim.'
— Dawn French, *actor and comedienne*

'You feel he lived it so richly, so dangerously to be so wise for our delight.'
— Dr. Robert Woof, *Director of The Wordsworth Trust*

'He makes it look easy, damn him! I couldn't put the book down.'
— Z. Menthos, *critic.org*

'Eloquently observant, beautifully crafted poetry.'
— Hannah Gal, *The Huffington Post*

LOVE,
OF A KIND

Achilles replied: 'Do not speak soothingly to me of death, glorious Odysseus; I would rather live on earth as a bondsman to a poor peasant than be king of all the shadows.'

— Homer, *The Odyssey, Book II*

LOVE,
OF A KIND

A BOOK OF NEW POEMS
BY FELIX DENNIS

with 66 illustrations by Eric Gill

Book and cover design by Rebecca Jezzard
Cover illustration by Bill Sanderson

B L O O M S B U R Y

NEW YORK • LONDON • NEW DELHI • SYDNEY

Published by Bloomsbury USA, New York
Bloomsbury is a trademark of Bloomsbury Publishing Plc

All papers used by Bloomsbury USA are natural, recyclable products made from wood grown in well-managed forests.
The manufacturing processes conform to the environmental regulations of the country of origin.

LIBRARY OF CONGRESS CATALOGING-IN-PUBLICATION DATA HAS BEEN APPLIED FOR

ISBN: 978-1-62040-626-7

First published in Great Britain in 2013
First U.S. Edition 2014

1 3 5 7 9 10 8 6 4 2

Printed and bound in the U.S.A. by Thomson-Shore Inc., Dexter, Michigan

Bloomsbury books may be purchased for business or promotional use. For information on bulk purchases please
contact Macmillan Corporate and Premium Sales Department at specialmarkets@macmillan.com.

For
Richard Neville
who changed my life
in 1967
with a bundle of
magazines

 Foreword

'Jettison the high-res —
Tell me what your *heart* says.'

his is my seventh book of verse. Just over a year ago, I suspected it might be my last. The last, at any rate, that I would know anything about — a fair assumption, having contracted throat cancer after fifty years of smoking cigarettes. My prospects, as the saying goes, appeared grim.

But then, I was born lucky and having responded to radical surgery and radiotherapy, I now very much hope to be around for a few more years (and books). That, at least, is the plan — a plan which also includes all-singing, all-dancing poetry recital tours for the UK, Europe, the USA, Canada and 'somewhere East of Suez'. The first 30-city such tour is being planned even as I write.

Of course, I have been too well schooled by the medics to do more than hope. As I write elsewhere, without hope we are nothing, even if the faith to sustain it is often in short supply. But it is the fragility of life, of all life — even the mightiest of mammals, a humpbacked whale, say, can be laid low by a microscopic virus — that makes it so precious and so desirable. How tedious our lives would become if we knew ourselves to be immortal. Uncertainty is unsettling and often frightening, but it is the essence of what life is about.

This bout with cancer was my third 'near death' experience — and by far the most unpleasant and scary. It is perfectly true (although victims quickly tire of hearing others remind them of it) that such events provide a fresh perspective on the world, no matter how miserable the treatment and after-effects. As to whether they makes one a better person, a better poet, a better painter or a better policeman, I couldn't say; but they certainly bring urgency in their terrifying wake, an appreciation of the immediate; of sight, sound, colour, texture and a heightened consciousness of one's surroundings.

'Nothing is the same after cancer,' I was told at the outset of treatment. Perhaps. At any rate, I dislike being defined by an event as much as the next man. My intention is to do my best to double down on life; which, for me, mostly means the making of money (an addiction I cannot seem to shake although I gave up smoking as easily as kiss-my-hand); the planting of trees; the writing and performing of poetry; the visiting of galleries, museums and libraries; setting aside more time to share with friends and in contemplation of the glories of the world around me. A solid agenda!

Why *Love, Of A Kind*? Well, because that was the name of the poem I was working on when a doctor asked me to sit down while he cleared his throat to inform me I had 'a sarcoma… a tumour in your pharynx…' Doctors do not like to use the word 'cancer' with patients, especially in the early stages, before batteries of tests confirm what they suspect. Who can blame them?

So *Love, Of A Kind* it was. As I gathered together material for this collection, picking and choosing from the hundreds of unpublished poems I have written over the years, the theme of the book revealed itself: 'Love, death and taking stock'. Not that I was aware of it until one of my pre-publication readers kindly pointed it out. None of the poems have been published in book form before, with one exception — 'Love Came To Visit Me' was in my first book of verse, *A Glass Half Full* in 2002, but I have added to it as the years have flown by. It seemed right to include it, especially when I was under the impression that I had only weeks or months to live.

One or two of the newer poems here, then, were written under the illusion of a sentence of death: 'Love, Of A Kind', 'In Flight', 'Alone', 'Last Request'. It does not make them better poems (one poem omitted from this book but written at the same time is called 'That Suffering Ennobles Is A Lie') but it does perhaps add a touch of macabre interest. Sadly, I have to report how repellent it is to discover just what a coward one becomes faced with what, after all, must be considered inevitable. The only decent response is to smother as much whining as possible and to thank your lucky stars you are not in so bad a case as many you meet in grimly cheerful radiotherapy waiting rooms.

I cannot deny that it's fun to excavate one's own creative past and to attempt the delicate exercise of rewriting, pruning, shaping or amputating: a task perhaps not so far removed from the surgery performed upon me at that Oxford University Hospital, (the John Radcliffe), in February of last year. So, yes, I have thoroughly enjoyed putting this collection together. I can only hope that you, dear reader, enjoy the result half as much as I have enjoyed its preparation.

The inclusion of Eric Gill's illustrations reflect the fact that I have been lucky enough, over the years, to amass one the largest collections of his work still in private hands. He may have led a reprehensible private life, (in truth, there is no 'may' about it, he most certainly *did!*) but as a sculptor, wood engraver, illustrator and typographer, he stands very high in the recent history of the creative arts in Britain. Talent has never been any respecter of reasonable behaviour, social mores, or solicitude for others. It was ever thus. And who am I, in any case, to speak of 'social mores'?

This book is dedicated to all those professionals to whom I own my life, from cheerful NHS receptionists, tea ladies and cleaners on the ward to an even more cheerful eminent surgeon, together with the department heads, technicians, specialists, therapists, administrators, doctors and nurses who ministered to me in my hour of need. And to my neighbours, friends, companion and personal assistants, who never gave up and were always on hand to dose me up, dress me down and bundle me into a vehicle for yet another torture session.

If there is one silver lining in the hideous process of being treated for and recovering from a catastrophic event or a deadly illness, it lies in being reminded just how much kindness there is in the world. The kindness of professionals and of strangers is a phenomenon unique to humankind; but the kindness of friends and of so many of those around me has been a revelation — one for which I am truly grateful.

— Felix Dennis
Dorsington, March 2013

N.B. Anyone wishing to read more of my poetry, both published and unpublished, or to listen to or watch me perform it, has only to go to my vast, sprawling, Gormenghast-type warren of a website at **felixdennis.com**

Bind Me To The Mast!

(The Plea Of One Who Fears To Love)

Come, bind me to the mast of thrilling hope,
Where I may hear this Siren ply her arts
  In sweet, seductive tones.
Yet, if you love me, loose no chaffing rope,
Her song is pitched to snare unwary hearts —
  And feast upon my bones.

I do not wish to love — nor chance the slope
Of unimagined shores, sans stars, sans charts.
  Thus you must lash me fast,
And jeer in bees-waxed silence as I grope
In mimicry of love — and all her parts.
  Come, bind me to the mast!

MANDALAY, MUSTIQUE APRIL 2, 2010

Voyages

The spiral somersaults, the sudden space;
The fearful, dark canals — the urge to race;

The pebbled rills and brooks of infant streams,
The cataracts and rapids of youth's dreams;

The first lone voyage as captain of the crew,
The stolen kiss — the secret rendezvous;

The anchor fouled on rivers in full full flood,
The halt to haul a neighbour off the mud;

The chartered middle passage in one's prime,
The grinding undertow of tide and time;

The ebbing shores of friendship and of fault;
The tidal tug on oars — the tang of salt;

The silted estuaries of age and sleep;
The fatal storm — the vastness of the deep.

DORSINGTON, WARWICKSHIRE   OCTOBER 9, 2002

The March Of Time

A better poet? Yes, perhaps I am,
But not a better man — the art of verse
Improves with habit, granted, but the sham
Of self-improving sacrilege grows worse.
We try — then fail to practise what we preach,
Our Damascene euphoria short-lived,
Fine oaths and vows are honoured in the breach,
The quality of mercies finely sieved.
With age comes understanding — fed in turn
By shibboleths, futility and fear.
The knowledge all is dust and doomed to burn
Is truth, but truth hard won, truth bought too dear.
    The march of time is measureless to Man —
    And none complete what mortal hands began.

DORSINGTON, WARWICKSHIRE   SEPTEMBER 19, 2012

4

'I spoke in anger...'

Easier cork the sea,
Or boil red wine from cloth,
Than rewrite history —
There is no remedy
To salvage shipwrecks drowned in wrath.

> *I spoke in anger to my friend,*
> *And now I cannot make amend.*

Better the tongue be still,
Than speak and then regret;
Better the bitter pill
Than wrath should drink its fill:
Some hearts forgive — but few forget.

> *I spoke in anger to my friend,*
> *And now I cannot make amend.*

MANDALAY, MUSTIQUE DECEMBER 26, 2002

A Bowl Of Quince

While things are happening, wonderful things,
Terrible things, things we shall not forget
For as long as we live, things to regret,
To be proud of (or not!), the so-called 'slings
And arrows of…' etcetera, the scary swings
And roundabouts of living — while we fret
That doctors may not cure us or that debt
Will sink our fledgling start-up — life grows wings.
For us, the world is coming to an end,
Our bitter tears and curses dun the ears
Of gods gone deaf, our guardian angels wince
To watch us build up castles of our fears
Or tear apart a clock we cannot mend.
Meanwhile, spring came;
                    a flower;
                        a bee;
                            this quince!

DORSINGTON, WARWICKSHIRE   DECEMBER 1, 2012

Out in the bitter cold of early December in my garden, I gathered a handful of fruit from my quince tree (just a low bush, really) and brought them inside to arrange in a bowl. All were pungent, some smooth and green, some yellow and blotched windfalls, more of a pear shape than a miniature lemon, some blackened husks rescued from leaf litter. How busy nature had been while I consumed weeks and months battling my cancer. The human sense of self all too often sets us apart from life around us, our awareness of mortality blinding us to our ultimate unimportance.

My Generation

I thought that I might be the first to fall,
    But not at all;
I buried them with saplings at their head —
    The cold, the dead.
The lonelier I grew, the more I sought
    (Yet never caught)
The murmuring of souls upon the wing.
    No bell would ring
For those who once had rallied to my side —
    To kiss, to chide.
Now I am as you see me, and alone;
    An autumn drone
Outside a failing hive of paper vaults.
    And yet, our faults
Were less than had we replicated chance —
    We danced the dance
Because we never knew the world was flat.
    We danced! Say that!

MANDALAY, MUSTIQUE AUGUST 3, 2010

Hollow Horses

None of it counts — not in a tinsel world,
  Where stage-struck generations do their worst,
Their followers' and stalkers' corpses hurled
  By ecstasy, or ignorance, headfirst

Into the bowels of what dead bards call 'Love' —
  Old Priam's hollow horses hauled to Troy:
The dead of night — a steel-shod boot — a shove —
  And from Love's side, an army to destroy.

MANDALAY, MUSTIQUE MARCH 28, 2007

The 'D' Word

I knew no father — nor much cared
　For those (it seemed to me)
Who filled the homes of other boys
　With wrath and tyranny.

I learned (and soon!) to stop my mouth:
　'My mother is divorced…'
Brought disapproving, sheepish smiles,
　And every smile was forced.

Still (true enough) with friends and peers,
　It set me worlds apart;
That 'D' word cleared a tiger's path —
　And broke my mother's heart.

MANDALAY, MUSTIQUE JULY 27, 2004

Impossible to imagine now, but in the grammar
school I attended in the late 1950s and early
1960s, out of 500 boys, only one that I knew
of, aside from me, had divorced parents.
I wonder what the percentage would be today
— and whether, or not, we should care?

'Deceit snares the deceiver. . .'

Deceit snares the deceiver
No less than those deceived,
    Liar and believer,
    Giver and receiver,
    Impartial as a fever,
Its purpose is achieved:
    When good men pause
    To settle scores,
    Or plead their cause
    By quoting laws;
    When trust withdraws
    It's head indoors;
    When conscience snores
    On tyrant's floors
And faith is left bereaved.

Belief salves the believer,
No less than those believed,
    Giver and receiver,
    Acolyte or diva,
    Implacable as Shiva,
Its purpose is achieved:
    When heroes rise
    In coward's guise,
    To steel their eyes
    At fear and lies;
    When weak men prize
    Deceit's demise;
    When love defies
    What guile denies
And justice stands reprieved.

DORSINGTON, WARWICKSHIRE   OCTOBER 7, 2002

What volumes of sanctimonious rubbish have been written, and are still written, about youth and its excesses. I'll excuse myself, then, from even a formal apology to the shades of Edward Young, John Keats, John Gay and E.M. Cioran for the loan of a phrase or two in this collage. After all, I am only 56 as I write this.

Leaving Sex Out Of This

Leaving sex out of this
There are few physical exertions more satisfying than
Taking an urgent piss
On virgin snow, or unwrapping a really good Havana,
Or lifting the first glass
Of nectar to quivering lips while leaning over the bar
To pat the barmaid's arse,
Or slotting an impossible shot — *bam!* — into that pocket
Your mates had bet you'd miss,
Or bolting two hot dogs with trimmings down your gob at the game.
Leaving sex out of this.

DORSINGTON, WARWICKSHIRE   MARCH 13, 2010

Soho Sestina

Champagne and neon bubbles frame the doors
Of yet another strip joint. Up the street,
Two constables are eyeing up the whores
Leant cross-legged by a wall to spare their feet.
It's early yet. A cat with bandaged paws
Is rooting in a bin to fish out meat.

Three sailors, on the scrounge for fresher meat,
Inspect the winking sign above the doors;
They stand there as the neon bubbly pours
An endless stream of blessings on the street.
The girls roll up their eyes in mock defeat —
They need a sense of humour, Soho whores

To ply the joke about "the sailor's oars
And Tiller girls". Plenty of time to meet
More likely joes. A scrape of copper's feet
And they're away, through alleyways and doors,
Gazelles in flight, up stairs, and down the street.
The coppers swagger by without a pause.

The cat surveys the sailors through its paws
Poised on its bin, as one by one, the whores'
Stilettos echo down the narrow street.
The sailors shrug and step inside to meet
A hostess, who will tell them she adores
It, even while she pours it — dexterous feat! —

➤

Into a pot secreted by her feet.
Her topless friends crowd closer as she pours
Out bottle after bottle. Back outdoors,
A junkie pimp is hissing at his whores
And threatening them both that he will mete
Out worse: *Now get your arses on the street!*

A prossie walks a john to some back street;
Slips out a condom, squats down by his feet,
Unzips his fly and slips it on his meat...
Then squeals! An alley cat with bandaged paws
Has brushed her leg! She flees. From fire doors
A bouncer throws three sailors to the whores —

Some early meat. A pause for blistered feet
From scores of tired whores in darkened doors;
But then, it's always early — on the street.

MANDALAY, MUSTIQUE JANUARY 10, 2002

I first came across a sestina propped up in bed, appropriately enough, in my Soho flat some years ago. I was recovering from serious over indulgence and something about the odd repetition of the lines helped to turn my attention from a pounding hangover. This was the first time I ever made marginal notes in pencil in a book of Poetry (*Other Men's Flowers*) as I painstakingly figured out the ABCDEF, FAEBDC, CFBADE continuum in Rudyard Kipling's 'Sestina Of The Tramp-Royal'. Said to have been invented in Provence in the 13th century by the French troubadour poet, Arnaut Daniel, sestinas have also been known as the 'songs of sixes'. Poets as diverse as Swinburne, Auden, Sir Philip Sydney and Elizabeth Bishop have turned their skilful hands to this tricky, intoxicating form. For my first attempt, which came out in a marathon all-nighter rush, I found myself compounding the difficulty by rhyme. It was huge fun, although the poem speaks of a Soho long vanished.

Elizabeth I to Her Ladies in Waiting

What gain is there from youth's proximity
While age endures the waning of the day —
Its once-proud battlements in disarray,
The white flag fluttering for all to see?
And what to us these minxes at their play,
The crafty wit of gallant courtesy,
Or mewling cries within their nursery
To mock this sullen siege of sure decay?
Best to be here, comparing wounds with those
Who share their tales of brittle bones and itch,
Old hurts, old skin, old agonies, old woes
Are more to us than rutting in some ditch.
    Old age seeks company to shield its galls:
    What might some hussy know of ruptured walls?

40,000 FT ABOVE THE GRAND CANYON   OCTOBER 4, 2004

Love, Of A Kind

She feeds
   her cats
      like Pharaohs at their altars,
She combs
   their fur —
      while chiding the defaulters,
She calls
   their names:
      'Come Romeo! Come Billy!'
She knows,
   too well,
      her neighbours think her silly.
This, too,
   is love,
      of a kind.

He prunes
   each rose
      with passionate precision,
He kneels
   for hours
      to weed each subdivision,
He grafts
   with shears
      and wages war on nettles,
He dreams
   at night
      of stamens and of petals.
This, too,
   is love,
      of a kind.

They blog
   the web
      as busily as beavers,
They save
   the world
      by cursing unbelievers,
They rave
   we should
      be hung and drawn and quartered,
And bid
   us drink
      the Kool-Aid or be slaughtered.
This, too,
   is love,
      of a kind.

We care
   for those
      who long for death's embraces,
We block
   our fears
      by lying to their faces,
We swear
   'Not me!'
      but yet our minds intuit
We shall
   not find
      the fortitude to do it.
This, too,
   is love,
      of a kind.

I wrote —
    but knew
        that what I sought was shelter,
I versed
    to hide
        from habit's helter-skelter,
I longed
    to love
        but cloaked my heart in armour,
I learned
    too late
        the coward's path to karma.
This, too,
    was love,
        of a kind.

Our lives
    are short,
        yet full of life and laughter,
We guess,
    I guess,
        that little follows after,
And should
    we find
        the ways of fate were mindless,
Why then
    regret
        a single act of kindness?
This, too,
    is love,
        of a kind.

MANDALAY, MUSTIQUE   JANUARY 14, 2012

The poem I was writing when diagnosed with cancer of the pharynx on the Caribbean island of Mustique. I added the last two stanzas just before boarding the aeroplane to flee to the tender mercies of the British medical profession. Normally, I would revise and edit such a poem, but feel oddly obliged to let it stand.

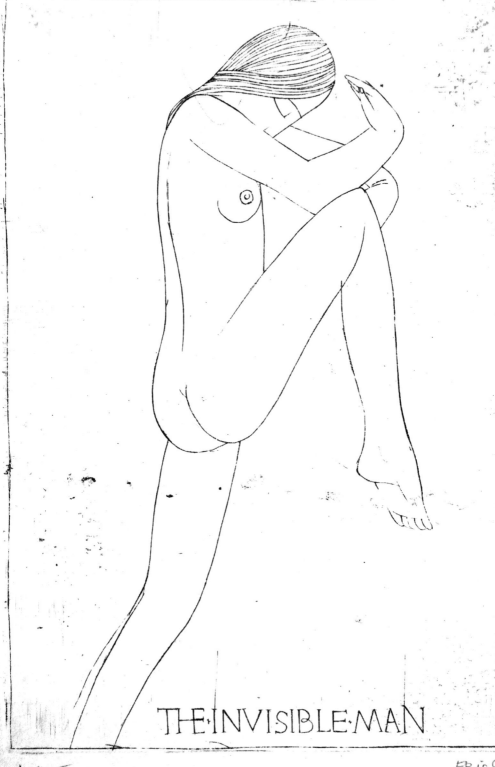

THE·INVISIBLE·MAN

4-25

ERic 9

One Married Man to Another

Our women seek to mould our wayward clay
Upon the potter's wheel of love's dissent;
Their tongue the whip, they shape us as they may —
Then wonder where the man they married went.

DORSINGTON, WARWICKSHIRE   JUNE 9, 2004

Loves Me, Loves Me Not

Into the ditch of sentimental rot
I cast your note and prayed the field would flood.
Not two hours gone — you'd pity now my lot:
Frozen fingers, up to my knees in mud.

DORSINGTON, WARWICKSHIRE   JUNE 12, 2007

Doubts

In certainty — the rusk of spoon-fed youth —
We dote upon a toy who primps and pouts;
    For all we court the Barbie-dolls of truth,
Grown up, we learn that truth comes clothed in doubts.

DORSINGTON, WARWICKSHIRE   SEPTEMBER 30, 2003

Crumbs of Comfort

How many crumbs of comfort — oaf!
Do men require to bake a loaf?
How many draughts of wine, my dear,
Will drown a fire and dry a tear?
For think on this — the rich can never know
Who loves them for their wit or for their gold;
And if men reap but what they sow,
Yet gold grows cold as bones grow old.
Keep friendships, then, in good repair,
We none of us have friends to spare —
And in the end,
Your one true friend
Is gold beyond compare.

DORSINGTON
NOVEMBER 19, 2002

'I envy them...'

I envy them, those nomad souls,
   Whose homes are in their head,
Who roll their eyes at stay-at-homes
   And fear no burglar's tread.

My shelves are full of ornament,
   My rooms a maze of chairs,
My cellar an impediment,
   My brogues aligned in pairs —

My desk an ark of trivia,
   My suits and ties and socks,
My rows and rows of darling books!
   My bolts and cunning locks —

I never learned the simple knack
   Of dumping surplus freight —
I envy those who scorn to bear
   The weight of real estate.

MANDALAY, MUSTIQUE JANUARY 3, 2003

Last Request

(For Marie-France)

True misery seeks little company.
For those who walk among the living dead
We know the knives of black eternity
Are solitary steel when hope has fled.
Even my faithful hound I subtly shun,
Nor can I bear the blaze of fresh-cut flowers,
I wish the world in shadow, grey and dun,
Preparing me for failing earthly powers.
As for you, companion of my heart,
I ban you from my presence, cruelly kind,
That you might keep my memory apart
From stenches, sights and sounds that foul the mind.
    This squalid end is not for you to know,
    My last request of you, my love, is 'GO!'

DORSINGTON, WARWICKSHIRE   OCTOBER 3, 2012

In Flight

After a cancer scare, flying from Mustique to Britain

So it begins — the last descent, long feared
Though long expected. Here then, in this pause,
Let me take stock, as if an angel peered
Upon my soul's mute rage and dull applause.

Come seek then, spectral dunce, survey the void
Of one who never sought or bought your aid.
Should all I wrought or fought for be destroyed
Can what is lost be less than what was made?

Omnipotent? Perhaps — yet I suspect
That time has naught to fear from men or gods —
The sham of cause is equal to effect
And Einstein's dice obey no law or odds.

Rambling fool! Bravado builds no boats
Nor plies an oar to swim some trackless mere;
Who sorts iambic herders from their goats
With hounds of hell upon the heels of fear?

Let us be calm. At forty-thousand feet,
Within this gilded bird's unholy pride,
No word has yet been spoken of defeat:
If loathsome Death may stalk, may Hope not hide?

And so it begins, the long descent to — where?
This flight from Paradise to homely hell
Is buoyed by more than wings, but less than prayer,
Too high to hear the tolling of a bell.

40,000 FT ABOVE THE ATLANTIC   JANUARY 16, 2012

After The Reading

Glasgow, October 2004

I had read my forty poems
    And signed the books they bought,
My wrist as sore as a toothache,
    My temper tiger short.

I thought of the pizza waiting
    Backstage, and stood, to leave,
When I felt two fingers sliding
    To freeze about my sleeve.

Too young for the battered wheelchair,
    A box of books held tight,
She tilted her face and mocked me:
    'You'll never get home tonight —

But could you sign these for me?'
    'Of course I can,' I said,
Lifting the box to the table,
    Wishing it were my bed.

And while I scribbled she whispered,
    And something happened then,
The room and gathering faded,
    The ink froze in my pen.

She magicked away the city
    And chanted away her chair,
The table had turned to a valley,
    The roof to perilous air,

While she sang me a song of warning:
    'We stand outside of Time,
But the gods of earth grow jealous
    Unless we speak in rhyme.

'For the kingdom of their seasons,
    Is built on melody's dance,
I charge you, here — be silent!
    And put your faith in chance.

'I have seen the ends of empires,
    (Of that I shall not tell),
I have stolen kings from cradles
    And sent their souls to hell.

'I have rendered women barren
    And stayed to dry their tears,
I have spat in the face of chaos
    Nigh on a thousand years.

'You are nothing to me but a poet —
    But a bard a child shall read,
I have not the power to stop her,
    Only the power to plead.

'Write nothing that might torment her,
    Of fear she will have her fill,
Yet in her hands she will carry
    The world for good or ill.

'She is scarcely more than a toddler,
    And you will die ere long,
But a line you leave will touch her —
    Would you sell the world for a song?

'Now plunge you hand in the water...'
    She formed a lake with a wave,
But the water was only a wine glass,
    And the book a barren grave.

I was back in a hall in Glasgow,
    The girl was nodding her head;
She was only a lass in a wheelchair.
    '*Thank you,*' was all she said.

DORSINGTON, OCTOBER 25, 2004

Dwellings

I dwelt within the shell of youth
  And thought to live forever;
But when I hinged the roof, in truth,
  It scarce kept out the weather.

I cobbled up a house of blues
  In Northwood Hills and Pinner;
Drunkards danced, but did not choose
  To buy me beer or dinner.

I crept aboard a ship of fools
  With freedom at the mizzen;
The bailiffs came with writs and rules
  And threw us into prison.

I helped erect a tent of bliss,
  Our free-love spirits soaring;
No sooner had we snatched a kiss
  Than innocence went whoring.

I staked a claim and dug a mine
  The fruit of filthy labour;
Then sat and watched the cables whine
  Above my hungry neighbour.

I built myself a monstrous tower,
  Its turrets vast and sprawling;
Alone, each minute seemed an hour,
  And madness came a-calling.

Bright bees of verse about me buzz,
  My hall is wide and handsome;
But handsome is as handsome does,
  With conscience held to ransom.

DORSINGTON, WARWICKSHIRE   JUNE 15, 2004

Frankie & Jonnie

Hackney 2004

'I need a fix real bad' she said,
Her stick limbs splayed across the bed.
'A *fix* — just one. That's all I need!
You got some, Jon'?' He shook his head.

'You know I don't. I got some weed.
You wanna toke?' She took no heed
And watched her hands begin to shake,
Uncertain if to scream or plead…

She yelled: 'Go get some then, Chrissake!
Oh Christ, I've got the belly-ache.'
He stood and growled, 'I'll go alright.
I've had about all I can take.'

He turned, 'I shan't be back tonight,
Frank' — all we ever do is fight.'
The door closed. 'Jonnie leave the light,
Please, Jonnie, don't turn off the light.'

DORSINGTON, WARWICKSHIRE   MAY 9, 2004

Summer Fly

He knows nothing of me, this fly.
Only the shadow of an arm
Blotting out the fine-wired sky
As he batters against the screen.
A flick of the latch — the fly is free,
Free for a little while from harm.
And is it not so, for you and me:
Fate intervenes, with hands unseen?

And what is he left with, this fly?
The lesson that persistence brings
Him freedom, that to try and try
Will take him where he seeks to be?
Yet if we know this to be false,
That faith will lend no angel's wings
Within the web of life's grim waltz,
Is it not so, for you and me?

DORSINGTON, WARWICKSHIRE   JULY 11, 2005

'Keep your soul in a suitcase...'

Words whispered close to my pregnant friend's belly

Keep your soul in a suitcase, neatly pressed —
An inn is not a residence, you know.
Don't kick like that, you're not a paying guest,
Besides, there's nowhere else for you to go.
No use protesting: life is all a jest.

Don't make yourself unwelcome and a pest,
The landlord's heard it all before, my friend.
You'll have your chance to get it off your chest —
If room-rates seem excessive, just pretend.
Enjoy your stay — and get yourself some rest.

DORSINGTON, WARWICKSHIRE NOVEMBER 26, 2005

'Inns are not residences.'
— Marianne Moore, *Silence*

Good With His Hands

Stacking the bonfire,
Laying the fuses,
Helping us light
The Catherine wheels and the rockets:
He was good with his hands —
When he took them out of his pockets.

Tweezing a splinter,
Sucking a bee-sting,
Heating a pin
To puncture a troublesome blister:
He was good with his hands —
When he kept them off of my sister.

Tiling the bathroom,
Fixing the boiler,
Coaxing a flame
From the pilot light in the Aga:
He was good with his hands —
When they weren't upending a lager.

Left like a rag doll,
Battered and sobbing,
Lying too still,
Curled up on the floor like a foetus:
He was good with his hands —
When he lurched through the door to beat us.

DORSINGTON, WARWICKSHIRE   OCTOBER 30, 2005

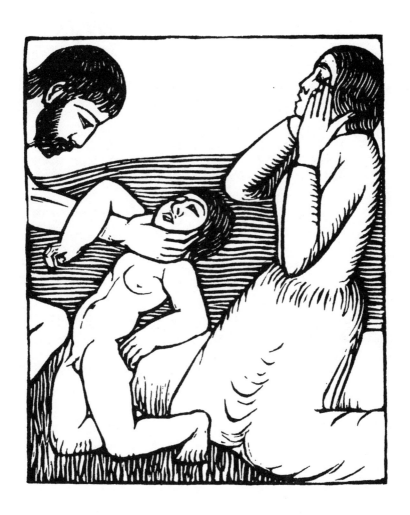

The Heart Sees...

The heart sees what the mind dares not perceive
And pitches camp when common sense cries, 'Flee!'
If sober thought suggests a time to leave
Straightway the heart replies, 'Where should we be
But rescuing ourselves from willful sloth
Which blots both mind and sense — as is our wont.
I know what you do not; forego your wrath,
Shall dreaming spires and vaults reprove a font?
Abide with me, acknowledging desire
For just this once. All common sense is blind;
Nor can it see each wish as gilded wire.
The heart knows what is hidden from the mind.'
 Aah, who would wish to know — for good, for ill —
 Tomorrow's fate today? My heart, be still!

DORSINGTON, WARWICKSHIRE DECEMBER 23, 2012

36

I Found A Spider

I found a spider in my swimming pool,
Unmoving — on his back. I thought him dead
And nearly left him floating, but instead
I fished his carcass, mumbling like a fool
(I dearly love a spider, as a rule)
Then watched, amazed, as eight legs curled and spread
Around my outstretched thumb, his silken thread
Suspending him to wave in ridicule.
Hurling ingratitude under a fern
I swam a length or two, then rolled to float,
Thinking furiously: 'You never learn!
Hearing a frog, you grasp it by the throat
To spare it from drowning. Ah, well-meaning flea —
You cannot save the world! Just let things be!'

MANDALAY, MUSTIQUE   NOVEMBER 17, 2012

I Looked At Stones

I looked at stones, but found no comfort there
   In hieroglyphic scrapings mocking sense,
Nor in the river's pebbles, long smoothed bare
   By idle streams of all intelligence.
      Even the henges, mightiest in awe,
      Have stood too long to open any door
When pointless pyramids entomb their own defense.

I looked at stars - past terror, past all haste -
   To contemplate what none can comprehend,
No messages; a vast and starry waste
   Spoke neither their beginning nor their end,
      But whispered only of futility,
      Immutable inscrutability,
Of void made flesh, flesh void; dark matter without end.

I looked at you. I watched you while you slept,
   The rising and the falling of your breast,
The tracks of time where we have laughed and wept
   Our little lives away in tears and jest.
      And rising up I cursed all mighty powers
      That what was freely given was not ours,
Not ours, but lent — such thieves! — at compound interest.

DORSINGTON, WARWICKSHIRE   OCTOBER 18, 2011

Some Promises May Not Be Kept

Some promises may not be kept —
Or should not have been made,
I penned this treason while you slept,
For as you bloom — I fade.

The squalor and distress in store
I would not have you see,
Better a noose than chemo's saw —
Live life in full — for me!

DORSINGTON, WARWICKSHIRE   OCTOBER 1, 2011

Please Don't Paint Me a Picture

'Jettison the high-res ⸺
Tell me what your *heart* says.'

Please don't paint me a picture,
Just provide the pattern;
Art, however skillful,
Trains the eye to flatten,
Lulling the observer
Into an illusion;
Set aside perspective,
Draw me no conclusion,
Put away your paintbox,
Spare me bright revealings,
Please don't paint me a picture,
Share with me your *feelings*.

MANDALAY, MUSTIQUE   AUGUST 26, 2007

'The world is round...'

The world is round. But not to me.
We each see what we want to see —
Tho' science shows horizons bent
Full circle, or a few percent
In colour photographs. But still,
Portray the damn thing how you will,
To me the world is thorny-hedged
With wire fences, razor-edged,
And in the meadow, fruit and vine,
And by the gate an ugly sign;
And in the stream a speckled trout
That men may watch but not fish out;
And in the woods are pheasants, too,
But these are not for me or you
With keepers spying round each tree.
The world *is* round. But not to me.

If wolves were born without the wish
To guzzle from a porcelain dish,
The rich are born with silk and spurs,
And sep'rate bathrooms, 'His and Hers',
While in their towers, wolves in suits
Export the jobs of men in boots
Without so much as 'by your leave'
So kiddies here must learn to thieve —
Not though they needed teaching much,
I'll grant you that, with drugs and such,
And gangsta sluts and rapper gits
Or has-beens flashing out their tits
On TV every other night:
No wonder kids think its their 'right'
To own each bloody thing they see —
The world is round. But not to me.

And I'm a fool. And old. And poor,
And don't know what an iPod's for,
I buys me bits at market stalls
And never visits shopping malls
And still votes Labour — God knows why
When all the bastards do is lie
And leave us here to rot and shrink —
There's more of us than you might think,
Who live in mortal fear of debt
And never surfed the internet,
With bitter hearts and brittle bones
And thumbs too fat for modern phones,
Who find it hard to understand
Who wrecked our green and pleasant land.
There's something rotten here. You'll see.
The world is round. But not to me.

DORSINGTON, WARWICKSHIRE   MAY 8, 2005

43

'Half my life has been in store...'

Half my life has been in store,
    Its fallen fruit confined
By paper twists that line the floor
    In attics of the mind.

Hoarded from the rot of cares,
    Wrinkled, dull, but sweet;
I haul my baskets up the stairs —
    The time has come to eat.

MANDALAY, MUSTIQUE   MARCH 22, 2005

There is No Future

There is no future — not for you — for me.
    Am I the child that stared into an eye
    Of glass sewn on my teddy bear? Whose cry
Would bring my mother running anxiously?
Am I the boy who hurtled, wild and free,
    Down hills upon a bike — who scored a try
    To win my house the cup we held so high?
Could such an athlete birth an amputee?

No, no and no — we shift beyond recall
  From what we were to what we think we are,
    And in our gross imaginings grow strange —
So Lucifer, awakening from his Fall,
  Stared out, a prisoner Prince of this dull star.
    There is no future — not for those who change.

DORSINGTON WARWICKSHIRE JULY 10, 2006

I Will Meet You There

As the veil of life's unmaking
Ravels up its thread,
At the moment of your waking,
When all dreams have fled,

Should there come a distant cry,
Or the echo of a name,
It is I — my dearest — *I!*
Though the sky itself is flame,

Though the hills are oceans breaking
In that last despair,
At the moment of your waking —
I will meet you there.

CANDLEWOOD, CONNECTICUT   JUNE 30, 2008

Pastures of Now

The field of Time has a barbed-wire fence,
    Thicket and thorn conceal the view;
Blind to our future — lacking the sense
    To piss on the Past, we stand and moo...

Slaked by the milk of a sacred cow,
    Chewing the cud of yesterday's grass,
Hedged by the Here — in pastures of Now,
    Lowing as carts to the abattoir pass.

DORSINGTON, WARWICKSHIRE APRIL 9, 2005

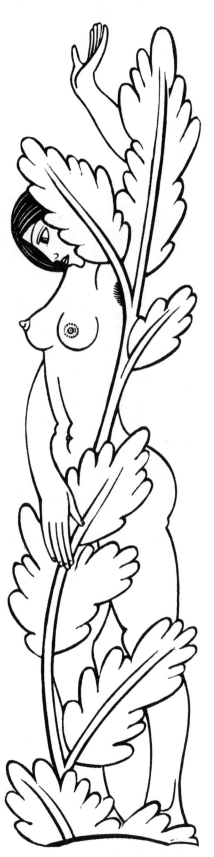

To A Child, On Getting Rich

Aye, lad, aye — the money's there
For any fool who dreams to dare,
As I dreamed once, when I was young:
Go to bed and bite your tongue.

Lucre's fine — a joy at first,
And yet its getting slakes no thirst —
I know you'll not believe me, boy:
Go to bed and dream of joy.

All its thrill lies in the chase,
Life's a journey, not a race,
The *chase*, my boy — and not the *prize*:
Go to bed and close your eyes.

Aye, lad, aye — the chase was fun,
And you were born your mother's son —
I know full well you'll drink your fill:
Go to bed, dream what you will.

SOHO, LONDON   JULY 21, 2006

49

Snails

'Quantum mechanics says that there are some things
that we not only do not know but cannot know.'
— Philip Ball *Critical Mass* (2004)

'Oyez! Oyez!' a modern crier hails
What 'any fule' like Molesworth cud have told us,
That as we stare at stars we tread on snails
And crush to shards the very things that mould us;

That far beyond the boundaries of sense,
Which quantum quacks now claim as sole explorer,
Our carthorse falls at yet another fence —
Tripped up by some new nightmare from Pandora;

For is not science sense by other names,
And are not 'senses' fraught with false perception?
No eye can see itself; why make new claims
For what the ancients deigned mere 'self-deception'?

DORSINGTON, WARWICKSHIRE MAY 24, 2006

Nigel Molesworth is a pupil of St. Custard's, an appalling prep school and the fictional author of books actually written by the Geoffrey Willans and illustrated by Ronald Searle. I was seven or eight when given my first Molesworth book, 'Down With Skool!', (Nigel's spelling is somewhat erratic), and this book, together with its companion volumes, has remained a treasured part of my library ever since. In my view, Molesworth, 'the gorilla of 3B', is a creation of genius.

'Nothing To Be Done'

To sense — to analyse — and then — to act:
As true for sage as blind automaton —
Self-flagellated flesh defines the fact —
A thought is transient — a deed lives on.

At least, we think it does, but heads or tails,
Who programs what — who iterates the whole?
If sense cements new bars within the jails
Of sentience — which warden feeds the soul?

And in what court of martyrs is it read
That ants may pass due sentence on the sun?
To sense — to analyse — and so — to bed:
But is it true — there's 'nothing to be done'?

DORSINGTON, WARWICKSHIRE MAY 15, 2006

Trust an erudite Irishman (ex-teacher) and an Irishwoman (writer) to nudge our dinner conversation into an invigorating trajectory. My thanks to Brian Grimson and Eileen Lawlor (both now passed away) for an hour or so of Samuel Beckett repartee — which led me straight back to his 'tragicomedy in 2 acts', *Waiting for Godot*, the single most performed theatre work of the last fifty years. There may be 'nothing to be done', but reading a play like *Godot* helps mightily to pass the time!

Two Left Feet

The laws of unintended consequence
Have nimble limbs; they mesmerise the dance.
With two left feet, our tutus make no sense,
For are not ballerinas born by chance?

Perhaps, but I shall share what I have learned,
The gods of fortune recognise no debt.
Bouquets strewn on a stage are mostly earned,
And luck is just a dividend of sweat.

MANDALAY, MUSTIQUE JANUARY 9, 2006

'I have been terrified all my life...'

I have been terrified all my life,
Though of what or whom I never could tell;
Of flying, of dying, of taking a wife?
Of failure, or was it — of doing too well?

We were a new generation, born
In the shadow of deeds we could never surpass;
Neither in valour nor mowing the lawn
With reruns of Normandy posing as farce.

We were aberrant, and saw no shame
In peeling a change on prosperity's bell;
Which of us stumbled through rubble and flame,
Or lay to make love while the sky rained hell?

We were the pipers of dawn and danger,
People of colour — and cripples — and queers
Outed from shadows, and far, far stranger,
Learning that they were our friends and peers.

We are the drones of diminished hives
Serving the Queen of an Obsolete Cause,
We have been terrified all our lives,
Of cancer, of boredom, and dead men's wars.

MANDALAY, MUSTIQUE JANUARY 6, 2005

Who Rules the World?

I rule the world: I am the cold
  Of darkness, ice and frost.
The days of the sun are foretold:
  I shall rule when all is lost.

I rule the world: I am the pull
  Of the moon, the tidal call.
For as long as the deeps are full,
  I shall rule two thirds of all.

I rule the world: I am the flame
  In a sun which has not set.
There was nothing before I came:
  I shall rule for aeons yet.

I rule the world: I am the breath
  In the scour of wind and rain.
Bearing the seeds of life and death
  I rule to shape Earth's pain.

I rule the world: I am its weight,
  The balance of gravity's sum.
The pendulum of idle Fate,
  I shall rule lest Chaos come.

I rule the world: I am the spark
  Of sentience and of guile,
Of will and word, of ark to quark:
  I shall rule a little while.

DORSINGTON, WARWICKSHIRE MAY 7, 2007

Tiff with a Mistress

(Little has changed in 100 years!)

Belay that noise! You think the money flies
   Into my pockets of its own accord?
   That any self-made creature can afford
To turn his gaze a moment from the prize
That you, yourself, so covet? Damn your eyes —
   Your very *pretty* eyes — my pouting fraud.

Assess this room! — its velvet, silk and satin,
   These chairs a master took a year to craft,
   That daub up on the wall (the fruit of graft),
Though gods themselves refrain from teaching Latin
To empty headed dolls — the bowl you shat in
   Just this morning, *mon petite*, is autographed

By Crapper. This very vase was once a Queen's…
   (A Queen of where? A Queen of *France*, you fool,
   Who lost her head and thereby ceased to rule,
As you shall soon — unless I find the means
To slip the noose when Chancery convenes.
   Old Goldschmidt's bailiff haunts me like a ghoul.)

Where was I? Yes. You find the subject dry,
   And yet you squat upon it like a leech
   To bleed out baubles well beyond our reach;
For two pins I would sell… there, there, don't cry!
It's not so bad as that… I've still to try
   The Beaumont brats, certs for a few thou' each.

If only Uncle Ned would speed his dying —
   There'd be no more of scraping round for pence,
   He's half of Hampshire locked in five percents.
Now dry your eyes — and while they're busy drying
Your boudoir calls, and you may practise lying
   In both senses, *mon petite* — at my expense!

MANDALAY, MUSTIQUE MARCH 17, 2007

What I Am

Success chased notoriety to bed
And what I am was born. They never wed.
Half-finished, asymmetric and unsure,
I bent the gilded bars to form a door,
Then stepped, a naked stranger, into life
And seizing Fortune, took her straight to wife.

Remembering the cage, I sought its door
And stripped it of its gilt — who would be poor
When riches can be whittled with a knife?
I scarcely noticed I had lost my wife.
Straightway, I lured a Muse to warm my bed —
And so the circle closed. We never wed.

MANDALAY, MUSTIQUE   AUGUST 5, 2010

Advice To A Young Girl 'In Love'

The more we know — the less we see,
    Each triumph of discovery
Leaves tangled manes of wonder shorn
    And strips a rose to stem and thorn.

Shy sighing bucks who seek your hand
    Soon tire of ploughing virgin land —
The wisdom, then, of history
    Is: *'Hoard each shred of mystery!'*

MANDALAY, MUSTIQUE JANUARY 13, 2012

Bits and Bobs

Today, I opened up a drawer jammed shut.
    A faded scent, where bits and bobs were kept,
Reminded me: that grasping, evil slut
    Was once my loving wife. And then, I wept.

DORSINGTON, WARWICKSHIRE APRIL 29, 2010

Writing Verse

And when you are done, more or less,
And the words are the *best* words in the best order,
As Coleridge put it, having crossed the border
Dividing certainty and guess,
And the words glow and the lines flow
And it is time for you to go
Far away and leave be,
As the wench flies free
Whispering that you can no longer afford her —
Why then — after — do you choose
Melancholy for your Muse?

Always it is the same, for me,
Providing I have not been idly faking
Or going through the motions with my making,
Or toying with my vanity.
When the words glow and the lines flow
And it is time for me to go
Far away and leave be,
As the wench flies free
Whispering 'The bruise will soon stop aching,' —
Why then — after — do I choose
Melancholy for my Muse?

DORSINGTON, WARWICKSHIRE JUNE 16, 2009

'Prose = words in their best order;
poetry = the best words in the best order.'
— Samuel Taylor Coleridge *Table Talk* (1835)

'You cannot live as I have lived...'

You cannot live as I have lived and not end up like this.
You cannot climb where I have climbed denying the abyss.
Long nights of iguana joys and terror on the wheel
Will lead you to a labyrinth where Minotaurs are real.

And there's the rub; for amateurs who act as if they care,
Too slow to cauterise their need to strip the wires bare:
You cannot waltz with Dracula then wave away the kiss —
You cannot live as I have lived and not end up like this.

DORSINGTON, WARWICKSHIRE   SEPTEMBER 12, 2007

Thanks for the first and last lines to Terence Blacker, whose biography 'You Cannot Live As I Have Lived And Not End Up Like This: The thoroughly disgraceful life & times of Willie Donaldson' (Ebury Press 2007) gave me, and hopefully thousands like me, such enormous pleasure. Try this quip of Donaldson's from the book's cover blurb: 'I am someone who always answers the phone at 1 a.m. because I know it isn't going to be my bank manager or the Inland Revenue, but probably a crack dealer or a prostitute.' Donaldson will be remembered most for *The Henry Root Letters* and *Brewer's Rogues, Villains and Eccentrics*. Blacker's biography does him proud – a gem of a book.

Guy Fawkes Night

The pumpkin moon slips under
A dragon's tail of haze,
In muddy fields and gardens
With matchstick men ablaze
We stand and praise
The alchemy of thunder.

A scent of something older
Is in the air tonight,
Far older than transgressors —
A reeking, ancient rite
To brand and spite
The demons at our shoulder.

As shell and flare are thrown up
To seed the sky with fire,
Our children clutch their sparklers
And wonder at the pyre
Of strange desire
They sense in every grown up.

Then somewhere, at the border —
(Of what, we never learn),
The roar of the crescendo
Dies slowly, as we turn
To let it burn,
The pumpkin moon its warder.

DORSINGTON, WARWICKSHIRE   NOVEMBER 5, 2009

There May Come A Day

There may come a day when you will call
    And I do not reply,
When seas run dry, when mountains split and fall,
When hell-spawned horsemen occupy the sky
    And all returns to clay.
That day may come, my love —
               But not this day.

There may come a day when you will reach
    And I do not reach back,
My limbs too slack to remedy the breach,
My mind grown mutinous — too dull to track
    The order to obey.
That day may come, my love —
               But not this day.

There may come a day when love shall fail,
    When we shall cease to care,
When what we share blooms colourless and stale
And scarlet passions fade beyond repair
    To sickly shades of grey.
That day may come, my love —
               But not this day!

MANDALAY, MUSTIQUE   AUGUST 19, 2009

Eternal Lieutenants

A flawed one — strong in the broken places,
Yet weaker than a babe in arms. Too loyal
And too fierce, just as a wolf-hound paces
Out the stag's last miles, careful not to spoil
His master's kill; wise in the ways of pack
And etiquette, restrained in his observance,
Eager for the pat upon his back
That tells him: 'Here is a prince of servants.'
Ready to bite; but not until the call,
Not until the word is clearly spoken.
Here, then, is one I prize above you all
And dote upon — the one the world thinks broken.
   And should he care, curled up about my feet,
   Which strips of venison are fit to eat?

MANDALAY, MUSTIQUE FEBRUARY 14, 2007

More Lives Than One

For those who live more lives than one,
Who live a life as I have done,
Where 'X' and 'Y' know 'B' and 'C'
But none know 'D' excepting me;

Their life a stone stripped bare of moss,
New ancient mariners of loss,
Cold connoisseurs of solitaire,
Whose laughter barely masks despair;

Whose sum is less than all their parts,
Who wander — homeless in their hearts —
Through others' lives, as in a play,
Who roam to keep the world at bay;

Who comet-like, delight to force
Unwary planets from their course,
Whose speech is consciously deployed
To camouflage an aching void…

With such as these — with all who nurse
This wanton, self-inflicted curse,
Beware their flares — and learn to shun
All those who live more lives than one.

MANDALAY, MUSTIQUE MARCH 30, 2008

Just Passing

We were just passing, so I said to Jack,
'Let's look him up.' We found the house and knocked.
No dice. I thought, 'We'll just check round the back.

And here you are. Oh, such a beautifully stocked
Garden — and comfy chairs on a striped lawn.
It's been years. Years! I hope you aren't too shocked!'

Startled perhaps, but not too much to mourn
The pink-lipped, wide-eyed waif who bedded me —
What, forty years ago? Her ringlets shorn,

The slight breasts blotted out of memory,
The flawless skin grown coarse — the slim neck slack
Where once my vampire gnawing made so free,

Her long legs scissored round my sweat-slicked back.
'We were just passing, so I said to Jack...'

DORSINGTON, WARWICKSHIRE   MARCH 15, 2010

Masters of the Universe

The land is now a bauble, bought and sold,
Though whosoever holds it is no king,
Nor conjures any Woolsack to their fold.
Sleek arbiters of greed yell 'sell!' or 'hold!'
And dangle lives upon a fevered string —
     Now let us sing:

    Fill up, fill up, fill up my purse
    You Masters of the Universe!

Sly urchins, born and bred within St. Giles,
Are paid a prince's ransom churning debt,
Canary tamers, fled from Seven Dials
To gilded City wharfs, sing out in aisles
Cajoling dizzy Prudence to forget —
     In soft duet:

    For fools alone would be averse
    To Masters of the Universe!

A fund of funds is managed by such ends
As few can either comprehend or know,
And those grown rich, to condescend to friends,
Must lead them to a hedge to make amends:
'Your pension's in the ditch, now watch it grow!'
     Fortissimo!

    My banker is my god and nurse,
    O Masters of the Universe!

But what is this? Applause turns to a hiss
And foul excess assumes the mark of Caine
As ruined lovers flee the Devil's kiss
And tumble, penniless, to that abyss
Where they must learn to chant an old refrain.
     Come sing again:

    As beggars all, now let us curse
    The Masters of the Universe!

MANDALAY, MUSTIQUE   DECEMBER 27, 2008

Aina

(Aina Vasilevskis 1952 - 2009)

Blonde to the bone,
Mad as a hatter,
Bright-metal Balt —
Mouth full of chatter,
Boa tattoo,
Velvet tiara,
Latvian ice,
Biba mascara,
Hasty when roused,
Motherly after,
Hands on her hips,
Rocking with laughter,
Amazon gait,
Valkyrie rider,
Seeking the mate
Fate had denied her.

DORSINGTON, WARWICKSHIRE   NOVEMBER 9, 2009

Plea of a Coward Lover

Fear, like want, is ever present —
Say what you will.
Emperor or pissant peasant,
Keen-eyed hawk or scuttling pheasant,
What is bravery but the skill
The strong employ to shield their fear —
And love the wish to drink our fill?

Come then my dear,
And need me still.

MANDALAY, MUSTIQUE JANUARY 22, 2008

The Past Is Never Past

The past is never dead, nor ever past,
    Its fat arse fills the room with stinking turds
    Or stands to slap our face with angry words:
A guest we cannot banish — or outlast.

MANDALAY, MUSTIQUE DECEMBER 30, 2011

'As I lay dying on my bed...'

As I lay dying on my bed
A demon raised his ugly head
And smirked: 'Before you seek the dead,
My chief demands a prayer.'

I shrank a moment in despair,
But then replied: *'And who should care?*
My sins are all my own affair...
Your master is misled.'

'Not so!' the demon raged aloud,
'About each soul, wound like a shroud,
Lies sin — and even one so proud
As you breaks at the last.'

'Our life is straw, the world is vast,
Time's breath a stream that knows no past,
Death's flag a rag to fly half-mast,
So I shall die uncowed.'

At that, he tore his mask away
And stood revealed: 'Then shall you pray
With me?' But I had nought to say:
'I know no prayer,' I said.

'I doubt it not, nor tears to shed,'
The angel sniffed — 'rise from your bed.'
I rose to find my fever fled,
The room as bare as day.

MANDALAY, MUSTIQUE   MARCH 13, 2007

Love's Pledges

Love's pledges must be neither
Too clinging nor too loose,
One suffocates in secret —
One slips the knot to noose.

When promises forge prisons
Love folds her wings from view —
Our ties grow often stronger
Than what we tie them to.

DORSINGTON, WARWICKSHIRE   OCTOBER 14, 2009

Cry All You Wish

Cry all you wish, my dear,
But not for long,
Youth has no use for Death,
Nor grief's sweet song.

The anthems of the young
Fuse flesh to dance,
The urgent lip to breast,
The thigh to chance.

No harm could ever come
To one so young —
Nor shall you ever know
The songs we sung.

Our passing is ordained —
The years fly by,
Weep all you wish, my dear.
Your tears will dry.

DORSINGTON, WARWICKSHIRE   DECEMBER 13, 2009

'No Trespassing'

Years ago, I found it convenient
To go about my business trailing
An invisible but expedient
Sign that said 'No Trespassing'. Impaling
This notice firmly to my persona,
I then experimented — reducing
Or enlarging its visible corona
To suit the circumstance, introducing
Exotic embellishments as required.
Eventually, this became habitual.
Results were all that could be desired,
Until now. Courting has its ritual,
I find, and will not proceed, hand-in-glove,
With a moonstruck electric fence —
        however much in love.

DORSINGTON, WARWICKSHIRE   JULY 15, 2009

The Harvester

'And who the devil might you be?' I spluttered,
  Striding to the stone-walled bed
At the bottom of the garden of my dreams.
  The kneeling figure cocked his head,
Shook it, as if a fly had buzzed beside his ear,
  Then reaching out, his fingers curled
Around the stem of yet another precious flower,
  Yanked it by the roots and hurled
It over his shoulder, the clotted earth spraying
  In clumps across the terraced stone.
The night air stank of crushed geraniums,
  Of fresh-dug graves and mealy bone,
My neat paths strewn with wilting blooms uprooted,
  Stems snapped, their stamens crushed.
'You bloody vandal, now look at what you've done!'
  I cried, but as I rushed
To seize him by the collar, he slowly stood,
  Half-turning, brushing the clay
From feral hands and spitting from his mouth
  Fresh petals in a crimson spray.
One glance into that white-eyed, glaring face
  And the cries died in my throat,
As he stripped the thorns from a straggling rose
  Bravely savaging his coat.
'All this land, this soil, this cultivated waste,'
  He growled. 'These useless labours…'
Jabbing out a leaf-wreathed arm, 'that could have fed
  My village and its neighbours
With maize and corn and grazing for the cattle.'
  He paused, and with a baleful eye

Hawked on a cluster of murdered delphiniums,
    Scooped them, hurled them at the sky:
'These… these water-sucking, pampered, pissant weeds
    That wouldn't feed a knock-kneed calf.
You must be mad, mad! All Westerners are mad!'
    With that he barked a savage laugh
And stalked away, his alien limbs still threshing
    As if to harrow the lawn,
Then vanished. Trembling, I lay upon the path
    To dream dry dreams of village corn.

DORSINGTON, WARWICKSHIRE   SEPTEMBER 29, 2003

Alone

Always, always, we are alone.
The solitude of self prevails
For worker bee or drunken drone,
In palaces, on beds of nails,
Worshipped as a new messiah,
Shunned as neighbourhood pariah,
Proud or fearful — on our own.

Always, always, we are alone.
Though our lover loves us madly
We are but a house of bone,
Skin and bone they'd die for gladly;
Sunk in cells of stony quiet,
Whirled in carnival or riot,
Dead or living — on our own.

Always, always, we are alone,
Flushed with triumph, broken-hearted,
Old and knowing, scarcely grown,
Blighted by the griefs we've charted,
Hounded in dark courts and alleys,
Bankers, beggars, Toms and Sallys,
Come the reckoning — on our own

DORSINGTON, WARWICKSHIRE JUNE 30, 2012

Inspired by *The Solitude of Self*, an impassioned speech delivered by Elizabeth Cady Stanton to the Judiciary Committee of the US House of Representatives on January 17th 1892, in favour of a 16th amendment and the rights of women in America.

Road to Hell

And what did we bring about?
The leer of a PC clown.
Machines that twitter and shout.
Swimmers forbidden to drown.
Teachers who bow to a lout.
Epiphany's throne cast down.

A cradle of spoilt intent.
A cuckoo who grew and grew.
The seizure of what was lent.
The silence of those who knew.
Whatever it was we meant,
We fashioned a world askew.

DORSINGTON, WARWICKSHIRE JULY 12, 2009

John Dryden could have told my generation: 'Your wars brought nothing about; Your lovers were all untrue…' (The Secular Masque), but we were too busy wallowing in Tolkein and Sartre, with a dash of Pangloss between tokes. Too late, too late!

'I Am Content.'

'I am content.'
Words I have not uttered these fifty years
And fear to speak them now — at least aloud.
So must I wait until a linen shroud
Propels me from the reach of gods and seers?
Yet what is lent
May be retrieved, and Fortune's arms are shears;
His jealous she-bitch messenger is proud
And may resent new joys in one she cowed
When all the world was young and me in tears.
Must I repent,
To choose between the sweat with which I pay
The tribute she demands from those she's kissed,
And freedom from what few believe exist?
Richer than any is one who can say:
'I am content.'

DORSINGTON, WARWICKSHIRE   JULY 13, 2009

The Fog Of Age

The fog of age begins as morning mist,
A word forgotten here, a name, a face,
Your keys left in the shop while you insist
You had them in the car. The extra place
You laid for dinner. Stopping in the hall
To realise you can't remember what
It was you came to do. The hopeless trawl
Through memory: 'What was it I forgot?'
Yet mist has its advantages — what's near
Is dearer to the eye and to the heart
When shielded from the clutter at its rear:
An April cherry tree revealed as art!
    The haze of later years brings fool and sage
    The clarity of limelight on a stage.

DORSINGTON, WARWICKSHIRE   MARCH 30, 2011

I Shall Be Sorry

I shall be sorry, but I do not care,
And shall not care when we have lain together;
What is sorry? A round mouth shaping air —

Thimbles of air. Well, don't just stand and stare!
Act your age. Untie this bloody tether.
I shall be sorry, though I don't much care

To know you cannot care. But I can bear,
This once, a love as fickle as the weather.
What is a promise? More mouths shaping air.

Hurry, for God's sake. Lead me to a lair,
Beat me black and blue with flesh or leather.
I shall be sorry, but I do not care.

Why should I care when there is nothing there?
The whips of love are lighter than a feather;
What is sorry? A round mouth sobbing air —

A busy thimble — sewing what we tear
From fumbled lives. I cannot tell you whether
I shall be sorry. But I do not care.
What is sorry? A round mouth shaping air.

DORSINGTON, WARWICKSHIRE MAY 25, 2009

A Patroniser Patronised

We lay at noon in bed;
   She turned and said,
'What is it (tell the truth!) that you are thinking?'
Hoping, perhaps to fish a compliment,
Or hear me say that soon we'd best be wed.

I frowned and scratched my head;
   Then turned and said,
'The condom split. A thousand smelts are jinking
Hell bent on reaching where we never meant.
So are you on the pill?' Her cheek blushed red,

She reached across the bed
   To smack my head,
But playfully, then murmured, eyes wide, winking,
'You think I'd trust *man*! Now, are you spent?
Or might I raise this nag to thoroughbred?

DORSINGTON, WARWICKSHIRE MAY 8, 2011

87

'It's always the dreams that damn us...'

It's always the dreams that damn us,
    Even the dreams of Christ,
Of Lenin and Quetzlcoatl,
    Of virgins sacrificed;

The dreaming of men of vision
    Who seek to right all wrong,
While their mesmerised disciples
    Salute some flag or song;

It's always the dreams that damn us,
    Of Newton, aye, and Locke,
For even the dreams of reason
    Refuted, run amok;

A man may murder his neighbour
    In malice or in pride,
But it lies with a true believer
    To dream of genocide;

It's always the dreams that damn us,
    Of Genghis Khan or Marx,
Of the caliphate, of Caesar,
    Of Paine or patriarchs;

By swords and the promise of glory,
    By pens of saint and thief,
By wishes that all should think alike,
    Our dreams bring only grief.

DORSINGTON, WARWICKSHIRE JULY 8, 2005

The Rill Of Hope

What feeds this feeble rill of Hope
Trickling to a Lake of Doubt?
Whose servants march beside its slope
Whispering of dams and drought?

From beck to brook, from brook to streams,
To cataracts of roiling grief
Which thunder through our fever dreams
To drown in pools of disbelief...

What nourishment from depthless wells.
From sunless seas — what nameless source
Dares circumscribe our private hells
To bid our helmsman: 'Hold your course!'

When all is lost, when terror reigns
And men despair — when deaths are cures
And rope the remedy for pains:
Still, drop by drop, Hope's rill endures!

DORSINGTON, WARWICKSHIRE   JANUARY 31, 2012

Without hope we are nothing. Another poem written shortly after the the diagnosis of my throat cancer in January 2012. I like Leonard Cohen's take on the subject. He once quipped: 'Sure, there is a crack in everything. It's how the light gets in.'

I Made A Garden

I made a garden on a hill
Beside a wood — it stands there still,
Six acres on a soft decline
Where Saxon once kept sceap and kine.

Within, I laid a maze of yew
To lose myself and wander through;
Then hollowed out, with cunning art,
New streams and ponds — then set apart

An avenue of linden trees,
Wild grasses, flowers for the bees,
An orchard plot of plum and pear,
And mossy mounds from which to stare.

The summer house I thatched with straw,
Then planted roses by its door,
And from that seat they framed a view
Of far-off hills that Housman knew.

Beyond the hedge for purple miles
Lay fields and footpaths, woods and stiles,
While I would sit within the pale
And serve my neighbours cakes and ale.

But pride in Eden bred conceit,
And though my garden was complete
I cluttered it with 'Wills' and 'Johns'
And 'Josephines' — each cast in bronze.

They cost the earth, or close to that,
Five million sterling, plus the VAT,
And though my daisies stare, amazed,
Now guards patrol where sheep once grazed.

I made a garden on a hill —
Ask not if I love it still.

DORSINGTON, WARWICKSHIRE   JUNE 8, 2009

sceap: O.E. for sheep
kine: cows collectively
A.E. Housman: 'Into my heart an air that kills...'

Meaningless-ness

I've lost…whatever… made me…me,
My song has fused to mime
Played out within a minor key —
More assonance than rhyme.

The colours of the world have merged,
They blanket me in grey,
The pain is mute, the joy is purged,
Each day an empty day.

The motive push of what has passed
Is laid in cotton wool,
My helmsman slumps before the mast,
Bereft of future's pull.

The voyage is done, but still the ship
Is wrapped in horror's fleece,
Dry-docked within its mindless grip
I pray for my release.

DORSINGTON, WARWICKSHIRE JUNE 23, 2012

"A poem need not have a meaning and like most things in nature often does not have," asserted Wallace Stevens (1879 - 1955), US poet and vice-president at the Hartford Accident & Indemnity Company. Stevens was 'one of the unchallenged American masters of modern poetry' according to Stanley Kunitz. Well, perhaps, but the indefinite article worries me in the phrase 'a meaning'. Surely a poem needs to have *meaning*, even if not a definite one. If it does not, why share it with the world; is it not simply the sound of air passing through a poet's mouth? The poet as 'Le Petomane'? As to the *meaning* of the lines above, I suspect they will be clear to anyone who cares for an elderly relative or companion — the human frame was simply not built for the majority of us to live through our nineties and beyond.

Bridge of Sighs

So many dogs and loves, so many friends
Have swept beneath this bridge to swell the weir,
My tongue stands ever primed to make amends
For any fault in reckoning those here.
For what is 'here' or 'there', and where oh where
Are all the golden summers we possessed,
The bear-hug grip, the kiss, the arching stare,
The leaping bark — the purr of cats caressed?
All gone. All gone. By incremental stealth,
By fire, by plague, by sword, by their own hand,
In terrified distress, in blooming health,
Black waters rose and swept them from the land.
    Their names recede, their faces grow more dim:
    What stream is this that none may learn to swim?

MANDALAY, MUSTIQUE JANUARY 13, 2009

10/10/10

For J StCB, PCE, FT, GK, CT, JC, AS, JD, PL, SM

Preposterous — I know it to be so.
A glorious day, gold leaves beneath my feet,
The sun upon my back, tall trees aglow
With autumn's alchemy; the soft air sweet,
The wind the merest whisper in my ears,
A church bell's chimes, the thrushes on the wing
And all is as it should be, save these tears —
As bootless as the source from which they spring.
I am a hard man, save when I write, perhaps,
Despising showy grief — *"I did not die,*
I am not here." — false sentiment that wraps
The hardest truth we learn within a lie.

    But ten in fifty weeks; lives ripped to dross.
    And now this ugly date to mock our loss.

DORSINGTON, WARWICKSHIRE OCTOBER 10, 2010

On Watching My Mother Die

I am no good at this — as bold men creep
From rooms where women dress and lay the dead,
I find that I have made excuse, or fled
When duty bids me face what makes us weep.
Cowardice then, for fear I delve too deep
Within those woods where bitter tears are shed,
Beside those crags where hunters dare not tread
And only wounded hinds attempt the leap.
Here is a lone wolf — long fled from the pack,
Who fears no mortal hurt or living thing;
Yet now, this flood of feeling swamps the track
Where I had thought to wander until spring —
    'I am no good...' I catch her flickered eye
    '...at this...' A smile, a hoarse reply: *'Nor I!'*

DORSINGTON, WARWICKSHIRE APRIL 14, 2009

The Lesser Lie

The symmetry of things beguiles the eye —
Each pattern of perfection flaunts a veil,
While blemished beauty tells the lesser lie.

A broken world was born that things may die,
That butterflies and dynasties shall fail.
The symmetry of dreams beguiles the eye

As art deceives the Siren's strident cry,
(All notes are true when sung upon a scale):
The arms of Venus tell the lesser lie.

A lover's arms shall hold you, by and by,
Though love is but a lantern in the gale,
Love's symmetry will blind the wisest eye.

Our wisdom whispers *how* but not the *why*
And forms of false perfection weave their tale.
While blemished beauty tells the lesser lie.

Nor can we heal the breach. Nor should we try,
The feeble stuff of life is grown too stale:
The symmetry of things beguiles the eye —
While blemished beauty tells the lesser lie.

DORSINGTON, WARWICKSHIRE   MAY 17, 2009

Stratford

Hours and hours today I squandered...
Here a glover's son once wandered,
Squinting at the splayed, half-timbered
Canted, tilted, caved, lilt-limbered
Dwelling house, its yard and portal
Mary's son long made immortal —
From these doors came William, strolling,
Sharp eyes in fine frenzy rolling,
Babbling from the Muse's lottery,
Cock-a-hoop to woo in Shottery,
Then to rue his lot at leisure,
London players, Fortune's pleasure,
Fate the bow and Wit the quiver...
Bless these streets,
      this town,
         this river!

DORSINGTON, WARWICKSHIRE   JUNE 9, 2012

Using a much later (and lesser — we are all lesser) poet's meter, 'Margarét, áre you gríeving / Over Goldengrove unleaving?' I write of another. The world is full of wonders, but the works of William Shakespeare defy belief that any single man could have composed them. As to Gerald Manley Hopkins, once I had deciphered his idiosyncrasies, his work grew on me as the years passed — and more than one poet has said the same. Any man who can invent a word like 'wanwood' gets my vote, 'sprung-rhyme' or not!

Oh, The Silk Of Their Flesh

Oh, the silk of their flesh, once hidden beneath
    Those mulberry bushes of plenty,
Their breast on my belly, their tongue in my teeth —
    God! What it was like to be twenty!

Sweet Jenny, Ornella, and Charlotte, and Blaine,
    In beds or on floors or *al fresco*,
The threesomes with Lily and knickerless Jane —
    Now innocent mummies at Tesco!

DORSINGTON, WARWICKSHIRE   MAY 6, 2011

Men Die Like Flies

Men die like flies — as they have ever done,
   And all our chaff of immortality
   Is gloss and glaze on Death's reality,
The plated silverware of races run.
What's done is done — and we are all undone,
   Our cruelty, our kindnesses and vanity,
   Our cowardice and talents and urbanity,
The love we swore would long outlive the sun.
Donne's 'Mighty and dreadful… thou art not so,'
   Rings subtly false, if noble in its power,
   And yet I think though men may beg and cower
Beneath the certainty of Death's last blow,
   Still, to have lived in wonder, hour by hour,
Is recompense suffice for mortal woe.

MANDALAY, MUSTIQUE JANUARY 7, 2012

This sonnet was completed just a week before I was diagnosed with the Big 'C', a somewhat
odd 'coincidence'. Would I have changed it had I known then what I know now? Yes! And I *did*
change it, but only the Bodleian Library at Oxford (which is curating my poetry manuscripts,
digital files and papers) will be able to decipher the original from this printed version. There's
a lot less bravado in it now!

Death, be not proud, though some have callèd thee
  Mighty and dreadful, for thou art not so;
  For those whom thou think'st thou dost overthrow
Die not, poor Death, nor yet canst thou kill me.
  — John Donne (1572 - 1631) *'Holy Sonnets'*

Last Thoughts
(As I Would Wish Them)

As lovers hasten clothes from off their backs
I contemplate disposal of this shell;
This carapace, which bore its burden well,
Is barred to mystery — too scarred by 'facts'.
The cloak is not the man, and yet it tracks
Those secret paths and contours of each hell;
The map of each man's face has tales to tell,
Proclaiming what he is and what he lacks.
Prisoners all, confined within a tomb
Of living flesh which 'Teachers of the Way'
Claim to despise, as if their mother's womb
Was no more than a factory of pain.
We fear to wrench the bars of our decay —
Courage, my soul; the wheel must turn again!

DORSINGTON, WARWICKSHIRE JULY 30, 2010

Ballad of the Goodly Fere
Part II

Simon Zelotes speaketh it in later years

When the Goodly Fere had shewn all false
Sin' they nailed him to the tree,
As the Twelve restored we roamed abroad
On the land and the open sea.

'As ye follow me now ye shall follow me soon,
I promise thee this,' quo' he,
But first ye mun' preach — all men to teach,
For the Word to set them free!"

So this we ha' done and the Word we spake,
Some plain, some cunningly,
I ha' dodged the stone and cowered alone
When fear bid me to flee.

I ha' walked the roads their Caesars made,
From Cana to Tartary,
We ha' shoaled the shores and plied our oars
Through storm and the grey o' the sea.

A gift of God was the Goodly Fere,
I shall join him presently,
For it's nay the scrolls shall save men's souls,
But the son of Galilee.

I ha' seen the water turned to wine
And the blind restored to see,
If they think to run from God's own son
They are fools to the last degree.

There are but eight left of the Twelve, I think,
But messages come to me
That an upstart hand ha' joined our band
Who was once our enemy.

I ha' heard his claim — the Goodly Fere
Hath spake him secretly,
He scribbles and scribes among the tribes
Who was once a Pharisee!

A son of Rome from a rabbi's tent
Who would set the Gentiles free,
I ha' read his letters to one o' his betters
And like not what I see.

The Goodly Fere was a brawny man,
He spake to our daughters free,
Who's this new cock to chivvy the flock
And crow incessantly?

He ha' not once met the Goodly Fere,
'No woman may teach,' says he,
But the Twelve ha' heard Our Lady's word
In cold Gethsemane.

This Saul, now Paul, is lately come
On a boat across the sea,
But he knew no fears by the crossed high spears
When they nailed Him to the tree.

I ha' stood my ground for the Goodly Fere,
A sinner though I be,
This know-it-I-all — this Saul, now Paul
Shall answer yet to me.

If he thinks to take sweet Peter's place —
He's a fool eternally.

Ezra Pound's 'Ballad of the
Goodly Fere' has resonated
in my mind for decades.
What a strange, sad bundle of
contradictions Pound was. Talent
shrieks from his pen and the
gods wept for his humiliation
after World War II. This ballad
was written as a hymn of praise
to Pound — a continuation,
however inept, of the original.
As to Simon the Zealot's
opinion of Paul of Tarsus, the
record is plain enough. Paul
was the self-appointed 'Apostle
to the Gentiles' — an apostle
who never knew Jesus of
Nazareth. As with so many self-
appointed acolytes, he sought to
reconstruct and profoundly alter
a message that required no such
interference.

See Appendix for Pound's
'The Ballad of the Goodly Fere'.

MANDALAY, MUSTIQUE AUGUST 14, 2010

• *Fere: mate, companion.*

A Fig For Prudence

A fig for prudence — half our lives are stale,
Corrupted with the mould of one another.
The sun still rises east beyond the pale —
Grasp any chance you have to seize a lover.

The eyes of the undead you meet each day
Provide the proof, their podded, fish-slab ache
Yearns only for the sanctity of clay:
What cannot learn to love can scarcely wake.

Pity them certainly, but waste no pains
To come to understand those voids of thought.
A fear of failure grips the nightmare reins
With iron force to spur such lives to naught.

Here is thy lover's flesh, forbidden fruit —
A fig for prudence — love lies at the root!

DORSINGTON, WARWICKSHIRE   JUNE 29, 2010

The Pestilence of Love

The pestilence of love invades
Both seer and fool alike —
Each bloody siege results in occupation;

Feigned indifference foils no blades,
No shield can turn its strike:
The only cure — repeat inoculation!

DORSINGTON, WARWICKSHIRE   OCTOBER 31, 2011

Desires

What you desire is my desire of you,
  That I remain in thrall — that tears be shed;
Such feelings as I have you misconstrue
  And force me to conceal, to gain your bed.

MANDALAY, MUSTIQUE   MARCH 25, 2008

More Useless Advice

Fear is the security guard
  You forgot to pay;
Thick as a plank, horribly hard
  But useful, in his way.

Rage erupts when anger turns
  The key beside his cage,
He feeds upon himself, but spurns
  To take a servant's wage.

Guilt is Mr. Hyde, the spouse
  Of foolish, idle tears;
If once you let him in the house —
  He stays for years and years!

Hate is hurt that never healed,
  Counterfeiting calm,
Grief, a wound where love has kneeled,
  Time its only balm.

Want supplies a heel with wings,
  (It never learns to fly),
Pandora's box is full of things —
  Better let them lie.

DORSINGTON JULY 3, 2009

The Oldest Error
To My 'Green' Friends

I love the earth, therefore the earth loves me.
You great green-hearted booby! All such stuff
Neglects what any fool knows well enough
Who farms the land or sails a treacherous sea.
We are no alien interlopers here;
Earth loves us neither more nor less than sheep,
Or marmosets or monsters of the deep.
We eat because our forbears dined on fear
And found it insufficient to their needs.
Fair nature sets few feasts for those she breeds,
Nor smiles to hear your Jeremiah groans —
This phantom lover soon will grind your bones
As she has ground all others, hale or halt.
Love nature all you please — but pass the salt.

DORSINGTON, WARWICKSHIRE   APRIL 8, 2010

The first line of this poem comes from an essay by Richard Jeffries written in the 1880s. Jeffries was one of the finest writers on nature who ever lived. His bleak, heart-wrenching prose on the English countryside contain such magisterial power that once, years ago, I closed the last page of his *Wild Life in a Southern Country* in my New York apartment, canceled my business meetings and called a taxi to return to the UK. As to my 'green' friends, I ask them, once again, to recall that Nature has neither asked for nor requires their help. She is indifferent, perfectly able to look after herself. As a species, we either learn to reduce our numbers and live sensibly or we shall be destroyed. It's as simple as that.

'The world was strange...'

The world was strange when I was young,
    Each hummock seemed a hill,
The names of things betrayed my tongue,
    A quark? A daffodil?
We swayed and swung from rung to rung,
    We wenched and drank our fill:
The wine long drunk, our songs long sung,
    And life is stranger still.

MANDALAY, MUSTIQUE JULY 31, 2008

When First The Game Is Played

When first the game is played, our frenzied limbs
Spell L-U-S-T in adolescent semaphore
As L-O-V-E; and though we now dismiss such whims
As voyages lost, their flotsam dots the shore.

Uncertainty defines maturity
And, in so doing, boxes its intent
Within a cage of false security;
While youth, though flawed, flags only what is meant.

Young love's armada seeks no sage consent,
Its need commands the Fleet to storm and wrack —
The key is what is read, not what was sent:
Acknowledging no signal but A-T-T-A-C-K!

All wisdom mourns the innocence it sheds;
The wise burn many lamps, but warm few beds

MANDALAY, MUSTIQUE APRIL 20, 2010

Yes, yes, I know it should be jetsam, but flotsam just sounds so much better. Try reading the line aloud and see for yourself!

The Pity Of It All

'Who is the man who shouts so loud?' said Danny to his Dad.
'A Minister of State, I think. Now change the channel, son.'
'What's that he's shouting to the crowd?' said Danny to his Dad.
'It's mostly lies', his Dad replied. 'Now change the channel, son.
    They must hold a new election, so they're swallowing their pride
    While they're promising the earth to silly sods they can't abide,
    But they'll sell us down the river, son, whatever we decide,
    And the pity of it all — is that we let them.'

'Why do the ladies shake their fists?' said Lucy to her Mum.
'Them's lost their sons,' her Mum replied. 'Now change the channel, girl.'
'It says they fought the terrorists,' said Lucy to her Mum.
'That's what it says, but who was which? Now change the channel, girl.
    When a soldiers gets 'is orders he must pack 'is kit and go,
    Though I don't recall Afghanis ever bombing us in Bow,
    And why the Queen don't send 'em back to barracks, I dunno',
    And the pity of it all — is that we lets 'em.'

'Who is the chap with chequered eyes?' said Danny to his Dad.
'That's Scotland Yard's Commissioner. Now change the channel, son.'
'And why should he apologise?' said Danny to his Dad.
'He's taking flak,' his Dad replied. 'Now change the channel, son.
    He's been busy chasing paperwork instead of chasing thieves,
    While his bosses set him targets not one officer believes,
    And he does it for the peerage they award him when he leaves,
    And the pity of it all — is that we let them.'

'Why do the children live in tents?' said Lucy to her Mum.
'They got no homes,' her mother said. 'Now change the channel, girl.'
'Why don't they build some? Makes no sense,' said Lucy to her Mum.
'They got no money, nor no food. Now change the channel, girl.
 They been slung out of their country though I couldn't tell you why,
 They say some of it's religion, but it's wickedness, says I,
 And the charities keeps feeding 'em, but still the kiddies die,
 And the pity of it all — is that we lets 'em.'

MANDALAY, MUSTIQUE APRIL 14, 2010

In her wonderful book 'Catching Life By The Throat: How To Read Poetry And Why', the author, broadcaster and producer, Josephine Hart, describes Rudyard Kipling's poem, 'Danny Deever' as 'a masterpiece of poetic, rhythmic perfection'. She backs up her claim with a quote from Eliot about 'Danny Deever': 'In the end, it is the pity that lingers.' Aye, it is. But that quote of Eliot's lingered, too, while the drumbeat of Kipling's masterpiece echoed in my head, until I rose from my bed and did what no poet should do in earnest — for a pastiche is not a pretty thing, however fervently felt. Even so, this is my tribute to a wonderful English poet and perhaps his best poem.

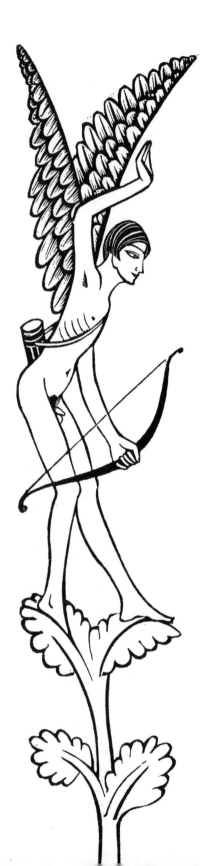

My Heart Is Cased In Leather

My heart is cased in leather
To turn a sudden blow
From Cupid's reckless arrow.
It was not always so.

For long I scorned the cherub,
Bane of those he kissed,
That quivered son of Venus
I knew could not exist.

He stalked me as Diana
Might stalk an antlered stag;
Now, hid beneath hard leather,
There lies a bloodied rag.

DORSINGTON, WARWICKSHIRE   MARCH 19, 2010

In Poetry —

In poetry —
I am the one I could have been,
The one I would have been,
Had nurture not dispensed with art.

In poetry —
I am the one who jeered at fear,
Who whispered in its ear:
Fool! Fight or flight is all one art!

In poetry —
I am the one I longed to be,
The sailor home from sea,
This chart, this compass, all my art.

But life is —
      not poetry.

MANDALAY, MUSTIQUE APRIL 2, 2010

This be the verse you grave for me:
Here he lies where he longed to be;
Home is the sailor, home from sea,
    And the hunter home from the hill.

—— from Robert Louis Stevenson's 'Requiem'

Sex Lives Of Mathematicians

Each fraction of infinity
Is infinite itself, my Sweet!
Mathematical affinity
As humble pi is easy meat.

Shivering flesh and eager tongue
Rely on no such guarantees:
Our joy is infinite — yet strung
On equilateral jealousies.

DORSINGTON, WARWICKSHIRE   MARCH 14, 2012

John Donne Sought Philip Larkin's Mournful Soul
(In Purgatory)

John Donne sought Philip Larkin's mournful soul:
'Well met! Thy tongue was foul, yet thou versed well.
What think ye, then, of Heaven's sweet parole?'
'You jest?'
        'Not I.'
                'Dear God, I thought this Hell.'

MANDALAY, MUSTIQUE   APRIL 8, 2010

The Devil Drives

The idlers seek the river,
    The merchants seek their hives,
The whiners run to mother,
    The villains sharpen knives,
The parasites find bunkers
    To shield their worthless lives,
Remittance men use flattery,
    To sleep with grocer's wives,
The pilgrims take the high road…
    But it never could be my road…
    I seek the do-or-die road…
    'Make way! The Devil drives!'

MANDALAY, MUSTIQUE   JULY 6, 2003

The Cremation of Jesus Christ

Caelan Fields, Llantrisant, Wales
January 13, 1884

Now stands the Old One, proud, on Caelan Field,
His Druid robe a symbol of his will,
The reek of burning flesh a righteous shield
As grim-faced peasants labour up the hill.

His outstretched arms a silhouette of fire,
He chants in Celtic tongue: 'Thus sacrificed,
I now commend unto this funeral pyre
The body of my son, called Jesus Christ!'

His voice rings out in agony and pain;
A burly smith sneers up at him and spits.
The black smoke roils across the sodden plain.
A farmers jeers: 'The devil's lost his wits!'

Alone, beside the flames, bereft of hope,
He hurls an errant brand in fiery arc.
Enraged, the screaming mob storms up the slope,
Their brutish faces shining in the dark.

'The land is for the living, not the dead!'
The Druid mocks, 'You have no business here!'
'Foul blasphemy!' The single cry is fed
By half a hundred throats as they draw near.

'Not so, you misbegotten Chapel wights —
For those who bury men defile the land!
I choose the fires of old, the ancient rites.
Begone! Or would you kill me where I stand?

'And was it I who saved your wretched lives
When pestilence had laid the village low?
And was it I who visited your wives
In childbirth? Well, was it I, or no?'

A rotten log explodes upon the mound
In showering sparks. The furnace roars anew.
The ragged mob has reached the level ground:
Their leaders halt. The Old One points: 'And you!

'Did not I save your daughter when the crones
Abandoned hope — and she now in her prime?
And you! Your broken leg and jagged bones,
I healed them; if you limp, still you can climb!

'Yet I am sore distressed and filled with woe,
My infant son, whom I named Iseu Grist,
Has given up the Ghost. I watched him go.
Fine thanks to bare your teeth and shake your fist!

➤

'Your Chapel *ministers* have urged you here;
Their only mandate — their *authority*!
I see they lead by *skulking* in the rear —
But what am I to them, or they to me?'

A man steps forth, his soot-streaked eyes ablaze,
A hammer in his hairy paw: 'Thou liar!
I care not what some heathen Druid says —
'Tis blasphemy! Consign him to the fire!'

Rough hands reach out in earnest as a shrill
Cacophony of whistles pierce the air.
'Police! Police!' the leaping shadows fill
With uniforms —
        I'll end my story there!

* * *

What's that? You're like to lynch me 'less I tell
At least the Old One's fate? Let this suffice —
        His holy fire judged legal — all was well.
                I wrote these lines to honour
                        Dr. Price.

MANDALAY, MUSTIQUE JANUARY 23, 2002

This is a true story. With embellishments! A plaque on the wall of Zoar Chapel in Llantrisant reads: 'This tablet was erected by the Federation of British Cremation Authorities, to commemorate the act of Dr. William Price, who cremated the body of his infant son on Caelan Fields. For this act he was indicted on 12th February, 1884, where he was acquitted by Mr. Justice Stephens, who adjudged that cremation was a legal act. Thus was legal sanction given to the practise of cremation.' An eccentric, brilliant and kindly doctor (one of the first to practise homeopathy and scrupulous cleanliness), an ex-Chartist who twice fled the authorities to France where he was forced to live in exile for many years and a believer in nudism, reincarnation, free-love and Druidism, Dr. Price was 83 when he narrowly avoided death on that fateful night. And, yes, his son was called Iseu Grist, Welsh for Jesus Christ. Sadly, Dr. Price does not merit even a note in major encyclopaedias today. His memory deserves better, although he must have many descendants if he was still siring children in his 80's!

Some Kisses...

Some kisses are like octopi —
    All tearing beak and suction,
While some are moths that flutter by
    On wings of introduction.

Yet others are a mother's balm
    To comfort or to wean us,
Those stolen — burn us like napalm,
    The venomed bite of Venus.

A tipsy aunty's are the worst,
    The bane of what they capture;
The best are hesitant at first —
    Then pave the road to rapture.

MANDALAY, MUSTIQUE MARCH 28, 2010

Parting Plaint

The future is forever in retreat,
To chase it is to race the rising sun
In marathons of folly and defeat.
Each sunset hammers home who lost, who won.

The past was once our future,
You would not heed it then,
If now is not the moment —
My dearest, tell me when?

You ask that I take refuge in our vow
Or dwell upon those glories soon to come —
A melancholy worm forgives the plough:
Your lie outwore its leash; my heart grew numb.

The past was once our future,
You would not heed it then,
But now is 'now or never' —
I dare not ask again.

DORSINGTON, WARWICKSHIRE AUGUST 27, 2011

'The cut worm forgives the plough'
—William Blake

Doll Talk

I know a girl called Jenny Bree
Who lives in Brighton-by-the-sea,
Her room is filled with dolls to hold —
Next year she will be six years old.

While Jenny dreams, her dolls discuss
Their secrets. Some make such a fuss!
'It's odd we never change,' one cries,
'While Jenny grows before our eyes.'

A rag doll clasped in Jenny's arm,
Whispers then in hushed alarm:
'You silly-billys, talk is cheap
But Jenny needs her beauty sleep,

So keep you voices down, for shame!'
A teddy bear without a name
Growls out: 'All very well for you,
But I have heard, and think it true,

That when young Jen' grows up one day
Then we will all be thrown away
And chucked upon a rubbish dump.'
'Oh, Teddy, you are such a grump,'

Chirps Molly with the bright red hair,
'As if our Jen' would leave us there!
When I was lost a week ago
She had her Mum search high and low

To find me or she'd *die*, she said —
(She'd stuffed me underneath the bed).
So much for all your nasty thoughts;
You bears are always out of sorts.'

A Barbie in a chiffon dress
Pipes up: 'I think I'd best confess
That once, I was her sister's joy,
But now there's not a single toy

In Susan's room, unless she still
Has Monty on the window sill.'
'Who's Monty?' asks a doll, wide-eyed.
'My bridegroom,' sniffs the Barbie bride.

On hearing this a certain gloom
Descends upon young Jenny's room,
Until a pony, soft and pink,
Neighs out: 'I'll tell you what I think:

I do not think that any toy
Belongs to any girl or boy
For very long. But that don't mean
They didn't love us, Jospehine.

I think that some are kept by chance
And others...' here she steals a glance
At Josie, '...they are passed along
To younger ones. I could be wrong...'

The bedroom fills with angry cries
As Jenny turns and softly sighs,
And all the dolls sit still as mice.
The rag doll says: 'Here's my advice:

There's none of us who really knows
What might be true when Jenny grows,
Nor do we know who made us all
Or what's beyond the garden wall,

But if I have to soak up tears
From other little ones, my dears,
And if it turns out Pony's right —
Then what will be will be. Goodnight!'

MANDALAY, MUSTIQUE MAY 11, 2003

Debts Are Like Babies

Debts are like babies — small at first
Crying: 'Feed me! Feed me, please!
You fill them till their bellies burst,
They suck your marrow to the lees…
But still they grow and grow — mysteriously,
And lead you by the hand to penury!

MANDALAY, MUSTIQUE   DECEMBER 25, 2011

My thanks to novelist Steven Saylor
for the first line of this nursery rhyme.

ET VERBVM CARO FACTVM EST ET HABITAVIT IN NOBIS

129

'Missing The Point' Pantoum

Why are you doing this? *Because I can.*
Balls! Any fool can say a thing like that.
Like what? I don't believe you've got a plan
At all. You're simply talking through your hat.
I plan to let it end as it began.

Balls! Any fool can say a thing like that.
Like what? I don't know why I talk to you.
At all. You're simply talking through your hat,
As if the speaking of it made it true.
Most speech exonerates what it begat.

Like what? I don't know why I talk to you.
A waste of breath, trying to make things clear.
As if the speaking of it made it true?
Oh, very clever! Mock away, my dear.
We mock what we most fear to misconstrue.

A waste of breath, trying to make things clear.
The clarity of words means what we choose.
Oh, very clever. Mock away my dear,
But you have yet to miss what you may lose…
The loss is less for those who volunteer.

'The clarity of words means what we choose,'
Is tripe. I don't believe you have a plan.
And you have yet to miss… *What I may lose…*
Why are you doing this? *Because I can.*
I plan to let it end as it began.

MANDALAY, MUSTIQUE DECEMBER 21, 2011

My dear Pantoum,

I know you are wonderful as you are — that is as a fifteenth-century cross-rhymed closed form from the Malayan peninsular made popular in the West by Victor Hugo. Normally, the strict order of each a four line stanza must rhyme *abab*, *cdcd* and so on and the poem must begin and end with the same line. During the course of the poem, the second and fourth line of the first stanza become the first and third line of the second stanza, while the second and fourth line of the second stanza becomes the first and third of the third stanza. And so on. However, when I learned that there are numerous variations of the pantoum still practised in what we are pleased to call the Far East, I decided to add an extra line to the end of each stanza (rhyming *ababa*, *bcbcb*) which is not repeated except once at the very end. As to my subject matter, it could be a lovers' tiff (Italic is packing to leave Clear Type), or me attempting to persuade my ancient mother not to cart herself off to Switzerland for an assisted 'final adventure' or the genius, Alan Turing, of Bletchley Park fame, testing the artificial intelligence of an imaginary computer. Or something else entirely, like a poet missing the entire point of a Pantoum. Take your pick, my dear Pantoum.

My Type

Of Gill and Goudy's classic spawn
It's needless to say more,
But Comic Sans and Trajan trash
Shall never pass my door.

For Dove, the font that drowned, I mourn,
For Baskerville, I rave,
My love affair with Cooper Black
Will haunt me to my grave.

The upstart Arial I scorn,
Helvetica — so neat,
Of Caslon, Wolpe and Garamond,
I worship at their feet.

Bodoni? Dingbats? Blur? I'm torn,
All Frutigers are ripe,
I dearly love an ampersand —
& Didot's just my type!

DORSINGTON, WARWICKSHIRE   OCTOBER 22, 2011

I've been in love with type design since I was a child. Of the few books I still own given to me in childhood, one is a hardback of large scale typefaces designed by Frederic Goudy. I spent many hours outlining his letterforms on tracing paper, eventually learning to wrestle with proportional spacing between letters — 'kerning' is the technical term, although I was unaware of it at the time. This skill came in handy in my teens, when I found I could earn money by making pub signs inked on wood which were required by new legislation to be displayed in all bars: 'Spirits in this establishment are sold at the measure of one eighth of a gill.' I was further delighted to discover that Mr. Goudy was no buttoned-down old grump, but a man with something of a reputation for fast cars and faster women. There are hundreds of books and sites devoted to the design of type (woe to those who mistake the use of 'typeface' for 'font') but as an amusing primer for the uninitiated, I would suggest Simon Garfield's recent book 'Just My Type' published by Profile Books in 2010.

(Figure 12 is a reduced copy of a 'John Bull' poster. It shows how the desire to arrest attention by making the letters as black as possible defeats the object of the poster, i. e. quick legibility. For from a very short distance the letters are indistinguishable.)

(Figure 13 shows a poster letter designed to give the maximum blackness compatible with quick legibility and a rational differentiation between the letters, e. g. the D & O.)

Eric **Gill** (1882-1940) English sculptor, printmaker and type designer, esp. Gill Sans.

Frederic W. **Goudy** (1865-1947) Prolific American type designer, esp. Goudy Old Style.

'**Comic Sans**', a loathsome informal face designed by V. Connare in 1994 for Microsoft.

'**Trajan**' a face by Carol Twombly for Adobe, often used by politicians and bad movie titles.

'**Dove**' a face cut by Edward Prince in 1900 and eventually thrown off Hammersmith Bridge by the owner of the Dove Press, Thomas Cobden-Sanderson — the bloody vandal.

John **Baskerville** (1706-1775) Birmingham printer and type designer of rare genius.

'**Cooper Black**' a fat 1920s serif face by Oswald Bruce Cooper, beloved by old hippies.

'**Arial**' a copy of the classic '**Helvetica**' created for Microsoft to save them paying royalties.

William **Caslon** (1692-1766) English gunsmith, designer of typefaces and founder in 1720 of the Caslon Foundry. The American Declaration of Independence was printed in Caslon.

Berthold **Wolpe** (1905-1989), a German designer who emigrated to Britain in 1935. His typeface 'Alburtus' revolutionized book covers, esp. for Faber & Faber novelists and poets.

Claude **Garamond** 16th-century French type designer associated with Jean **Jannon.**

Giambattista **Bodoni** (1740-1813) Brilliant Italian type designer, a rival to **Didot** (see below).

Zapf '**Dingbats**', a typeface of symbols by 20th-century German designer Hermann Zapf.

'**Blur**' a face designed by Neville Brody, arguably Britain's finest living graphic designer.

Adrian **Frutiger**, influential 20th-century Swiss type designer, esp. 'Univers' and 'Frutiger'.

Firmin **Didot**, late 18th-century printer and type founder whose hairline serifs still dazzle.

Enough

I wish you enough of a summer sun's measure
   To savour an apple tree's shade,
Enough of the mischief of youth and its pleasure
   For silence when others have strayed.

I wish you enough of the wisdom of learning
   To challenge the truths of the wise,
Enough of the road and a vagabond's yearning
   To wander and wear out your eyes.

I wish you enough of the madness of wooing
   As lusting and loving collide,
Enough of the blindness that shadows pursuing
   To bind you as passions subside.

I wish you enough of your getting and giving
   To fathom the value of both,
Enough of betrayal to grasp that forgiving
   Annuls any promise or oath.

I wish you enough of the kindness of others
   To temper the powers you wield,
Enough of the love of your sisters and brothers
   To barter your blade for a shield.

I wish you enough of the healing of laughter
   To bury each grief in its day,
Enough of forbearance, both here and hereafter,
   To wink at each dragon you slay.

I wish you enough of this life's Bacchanalia
   To swallow the sweet with the rough,
To gorge on the glories of triumph — and failure!
   Until your heart whispers: 'Enough!'

DORSINGTON, WARWICKSHIRE   JULY 19, 2011

We Are All Bede's Bird

We are all Bede's bird.
Darting into a hall of light
One frozen, solitary night
To find to our astonishment
A world of warmth, of wonderment,
Awash with sounds that shake our frame
And things for which we have no name,
Our flight too fast to bank or stall,
We sheer across the feasting hall
And out into the frozen sky,
Some say to live, some say to die,
(And some that we've not flown at all,
But simply dreamt up feast and hall...)
Though all agree, once out the door
The sparrow may return no more —
It seems absurd, but I have heard
Brave men have died to pass The Word
That we are all Bede's bird.

DORSINGTON, WARWICKSHIRE JULY 5, 2011

'Such,' he said, 'O King, seems to me the present life of men on earth, in comparison with that time which to us is uncertain, as if when on a winter's night you sit feasting with your earldormen and brumali, and a simple sparrow should fly into the hall, and coming in at one door, instantly fly out through another. In that time in which it is indoors it is indeed not touched by the fury of the winter; but yet, this smallest space of calmness being passed almost in a flash, from winter going into winter again, it is lost to our eyes. Somewhat like this appears the life of man, but of what follows or what went before, we are utterly ignorant.' — The Venerable Bede 'Ecclesiastical History', Book II 731 A.D. the story of the consultation between Edwin of Northumbria and his nobles whether they shall accept the missionary gospel as preached by Paulinus.

You think you see

You think you see, and yet your eyes are blind.
They fix upon the screens of what you were
Or what you have become, each scene confined
To galaxies of flesh, or fin, or fur.
You see as flies see: partial, sharp and skewed,
The gross minutiae of turds or lust,
Discoloured by the vagaries of mood,
Of need, forbidden joys and self-disgust.
An artist dare not trust — he seeks to tear
All veils to ragged shreds and cast them down.
Behold the blank abyss! The Gaza stare!
The Parthenon reduced to shantytown!
    The soul of art lies not in what we make,
    But in the void of what we dare forsake.

MANDALAY, MUSTIQUE   JANUARY 18, 2010

Exit, pursued by a bear...

When you dare not dry a china dish
    for fear you cannot catch it,
When you're slow to take a tenner out
    for fear a yob will snatch it;

When you turn the television on
    and everything's offensive,
When your home is worth a fortune
    but a loaf is so expensive;

When you leave the bathroom door ajar
    in case they cannot reach you,
When you'd like to try computers,
    but there's nobody to teach you;

When you've long outlived the doctor
    with his farcical prognosis,
When your single living enemy
    is osteoporosis;

When your friends laid in their coffins
    look much happier than you do,
When your children speak Swahili and
    their spouses practise voodoo;

When attire is back in fashion you
    abandoned in your forties,
When your shopping expeditions turn
    to military sorties;

When your spectacles go walk-about
    upon a daily basis,
When your house becomes a fortress
    and your garden an oasis;

When you can't remember what it was
    you made yourself for supper,
When there's sugar in the kitty's bowl
    and cat food in your cuppa;

When those kindly meaning ladies from
   the Council call you 'dearie',
When they speak about a 'living will',
   and all the world grows weary;

Then it's time to book a life-time's cruise,
   Although the prospect scares you:
And be sure to sail first class, my dear —
   Unless you wish your heirs to!

DORSINGTON, WARWICKSHIRE   APRIL 17, 2005

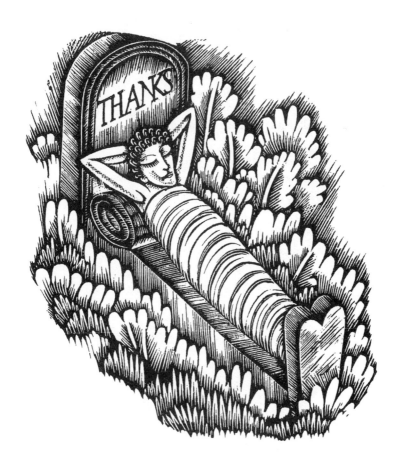

The Child Within

If I could only root within
This miser's hoard of joy and sin
Stored up inside my memory;

To view at leisure things forgot,
To sort what *was* from what was *not*
Inside this vast ephemery,

Before the carapace of youth
Had hardened into knowing truth
And flattered every foe I fought;

To search, with nothing left to prove,
To excavate, at one remove,
All that I felt, all that I thought;

To bribe the guards of vanity
And snap the mask of sanity
From off my face. A sweet release!

For but a week, for but one hour,
To pacify, with all my power,
The child within
      — and make my peace.

MANDALAY, MUSTIQUE JANUARY 23, 2003

To Look And See

I like to look at things, to look and see —
The pattern left by brushes buffing suede;
Blonde eyelashes on pigs; the history
Of furniture that wax and use have made;

The mirror of the sky's strange alchemy
As clouds breed crawling colonies of shade;
A film of pollen dusted on a bee;
White mould within old jars of marmalade;

The hues of peeling bark upon a tree;
The knowing eyes of statues long decayed;
The sickly sheen of oil spilt in the sea;
The arc of craftsmen brandishing a blade;

Hang up dull Habit's blindfold on its hook —
Let's look and look to *see*, not just to look.

DORSINGTON, WARWICKSHIRE   MAY 15, 2011

What Do We Owe The Dead?

What do we owe the dead
   When leaden night has claimed them,
When flesh and word have fled,
   And memory has framed them?
      To speak no ill,
      To shield them still,
    To veil their misdemeanors
      From disrepute,
      To substitute
    Chihuahuas for hyenas?
What do we owe the dead
   When flame or dust has claimed them,
When all excuse is fled
   And martyr's light has framed them?

What do we owe to whom,
   Their kin — their friends — their lovers?
Shall history presume
   That truth must trump all others —
      No stone unturned,
      No diary burned,
    No papers left encoded,
      No kindly vault
      To shutter fault —
    No smoking gun unloaded?
What do we owe the dead
   When those in trust have shamed them,
When all excuse is fled,
   And tribe or scribe has claimed them?

DORSINGTON, WARWICKSHIRE JULY 5, 2011

The metre and rhyme-scheme for this poem comes from 'Oft In The Stilly Night' by Thomas Moore (1779 - 1852). The son of a Dublin grocer, Moore became a successful poet and singer, known chiefly for his 'Poems', published in 1801, and his even more successful 'Irish Melodies'. Lord Byron entrusted his unpublished 'Memoirs' to Moore with instructions to publish it following his (Byron's) death. After first selling the manuscript to a bookseller for 2,000 guineas, Moore had second thoughts and borrowed a small fortune to reclaim it. He then claimed to have burnt the manuscript. Not all literary sleuths are convinced he did so and harbour hopes that one day this sensational document may come to light. It was the apparent breach of trust by Moore which suggested the title and theme of this poem to me. Undoubtedly, he did what he did to protect the reputation of his friend. What, indeed, do we owe the dead?

'Who was I then...?'

Who was I then, when first I learned
That not all pages can be turned;
That not all things can be set right;
That neither love nor luck is earned?

When was it that I first took fright,
And begged them to leave on the light;
Or prayed in bed for God to keep
A mighty sinner safe that night?

Whose widened eyes, too dry to weep,
Sowed memories for me to reap?
Who gripped a ragged teddy's arm
And sought to slay the dragon Sleep?

Who whispers now in crazed alarm
Those infant oaths, sealed palm to palm,
Those promises to do least harm?
That each to each must do least harm.

DORSINGTON, WARWICKSHIRE   27 SEPTEMBER, 2005

If the past is a different country, then far from the child being 'father of the Man',
is it not more likely that the child is an absolute stranger to its grown self?

Illustrated Apes

An ochre bison shuffles from the stone,
    Preserved in darkness, pigment mimics bone;
If farmers push the plough that oxen pull,
    Which, then, the matador, and which the bull?

White beards have preached the coming of messiahs
    Since illustrated apes sketched their desires;
But then — so many gods have served our needs,
    What matters is it which a sinner pleads?

Art dances in a ring while empires rust,
    And dances on — while each is ground to dust;
Within these timeless caves, an ochre sign:
        'HERE,
        ILLUSTRATED APES
        ONCE DREW A LINE.'

DORSINGTON, WARWICKSHIRE SEPTEMBER 5, 2005

Faith And Hope

Faith is armoured, girt for war,
Certain of one creed, one law.
Hope stands naked — and unsure.

Faith seeks sinners to retrieve,
Flaying those that disbelieve.
Hope seems helpless — and naive.

Yet the brightest steel may rust,
Faithless gods return to dust.
Hope outlives all things — in trust.

DORSINGTON, WARWICKSHIRE   MAY 8, 2011

The First Of May

Hooray! Hooray! the first of May,
Outdoor fucking starts today,
But insulate your derriéres
Unless you're ducks or polar bears.

The rain is wet, the wind will freeze
All manner of extremities,
Best wait for June to rut and rout,
And cast no clout 'til May is out!

DORSINGTON, WARWICKSHIRE
MAY 1, 2011

clout: (noun) archaic
piece of cloth or
article of clothing

The Beast Within

The beast within, which men believe they cage,
Is not the loathsome creature we surmise,
Some dark monstrosity with blood-dimmed eyes,
Quiescent, save when anger seeps to rage.
No subterranean landscape lurks backstage,
Those tapestries of id in stormy skies
That Sigmund conjured whole — his ego's prize!
Beware the gifts of princes, or the sage.
For you — and you alone — stride on this sphere,
All others are but shadows in your path,
The dark imaginings of love and wrath
Which you — and you alone — have conjured here:
The grapes of fear and hurt on which we feast
Are spectres in the wind. We *are* the beast!

MANDALAY, MUSTIQUE   APRIL 7, 2010

A Flawed Rose

What perfect Juliet or Mr. Right
Ever drew breath? Trust me in this, my dear.
No sooner do such paragons appear
And sweep us from our eager feet one night
To realms of shuddering bliss and stunned delight,
Than imperfections creep upon the ear
Or eye. Even as longing draws us near,
Some blemish brings them tumbling from their height.
Nor can we leaven heartbreak with surprise:
Who was it placed them on a pedestal,
These idols unalloyed? Desire bred lies
As surely as our blindness fuelled their fall.
The thorns of compromise are no great blights —
Better a half-flawed rose than lonely nights.

DORSINGTON, WARWICKSHIRE   MARCH 13, 2010

'Thank You'

To those who nudge and wink, to toad and schemer
 Who earlier had praised you fast enough,
To those who croak: 'Another bloody dreamer...'
 And turn away when things are getting tough,
To false fair-weather friends who thought you barmy,
 Each praying you would fail and prove 'em right,
Or Jeremiah fools — that closet army
 Of wretches with no stomach for the fight;

To twenty-twenty hindsight from your lenders
 Who panicked at each petty storm or squall,
To those you once had thought were your defenders,
 But oddly will no longer take your call,
To bottom-feeding scum who would defraud you
 Like pirates, for a penny in the pound,
Or those who speak of life-boats as they board you
 To rob you just the second you're aground;

To Nightmare and his cohorts that come creeping
 In fevered dreams of loss beyond repair,
To thudding heart and night sweats as you're sleeping
 While Fear incites fresh servants of Despair,
To doubts that stride by daylight to assail you
 And stop your mouth with thoughts of the abyss,
Or siren sighs whose whisperings impale you:
 'My dearest, I implore you, drop all this...'

To ghouls who cram their gullets with your winnings
 And pass the bottle round in loud salute,
To creeps who claim they 'nurtured your beginnings',
 (A bone they tossed, and grudgingly, to boot),
To those who claim your bed, your gifts, your riches
 Now Lady Luck has brought you safe to port,
Say 'thank you' — as you bless the sons-of-bitches
 For every rotten trick the buggers taught!

DORSINGTON, WARWICKSHIRE APRIL 21, 2011

With apologies to the immortal Rudyard Kipling

The domestic hose comes out well in time of drought

The Rewards of Winter Gardening

'You smell of man,' she said.
'What's that?' 'God knows.
Old woodsmoke, recent sweat; the hides of cows.'
'I'll take a shower,' I said,
'And change these clothes.'
'Not yet you fool!' — unbuttoning her blouse.

DORSINGTON, WARWICKSHIRE FEBRUARY 7, 2010

'I am fleeing for my life...'

I am fleeing for my life — or maybe from it —
'The thief doth fear each bush an officer',
The years have seared the stars since Halley's comet
And neither speed nor wind are what they were
When adolescent lungs were near immortal,
When muscle, flesh and bone were knitted steel:
I am fleeing for my life, though through which portal
I little know or care — nor which is 'real'.

I am emptying the wine from life's decanter —
While musing, 'Do I dare?' each glass I pour;
I have grown too fond of gallows-haunted banter,
Nor am I quite as knowing as before,
For the laughter of the gods grows ever louder
And I mark the rents through which their weary eyes
Peer down upon this world of paint and powder,
Where nothing is as kind as it is wise.

I am learning to wear purple and surround it
With rhyme-edged braid to urge the world to waltz:
Should I leave it one whit better than I found it,
What of it, when all scenery is false?
I have gifted them a forest; who shall ward it
Through storm, through blast, shall owe no debt to me:
I am fleeing for my life — or else toward it —
And little know or care which one it be.

DORSINGTON, WARWICKSHIRE MARCH 29, 2009

Suspicion always haunts the guilty mind;
The thief doth think each bush an officer.
    ——William Shakespeare Henry VI, Pt 3

   And indeed there will be time
To wonder, 'Do I dare?' and, 'Do I dare?'
Time to turn back and descend the stair...
    —— from 'The Love Song of J. Alfred Prufrock' by T. S. Eliot

When I am an old woman I shall wear purple
With a red hat which doesn't go, and doesn't suit me.
    —— from 'Warning' by Jenny Joseph

Not in Vain

Not in vain are tears or petals shed,
They fall to still their hungry mother's pain;
The stuff of life is built upon the dead.

The bones of monsters leach our daily bread,
The blood of kings runs riot in each vein,
Not in vain are tears or petals shed.

If nightingales now sing where Sappho fled,
A poet chants within that lost refrain;
Our art is but the salvage of the dead.

The borrowed air we breathe, the earth we tread,
The spittle in our mouths that fell as rain;
Not in vain are tears or petals shed.

The plains of joy, the dark defiles of dread,
Are stitched upon the maps of Death's domain;
Our patchwork paths are quilted by the dead,

Their rags of life respun as golden thread.
Nothing ever lost is lost in vain,
And not in vain are tears or petals shed:
The stuff of life is built upon the dead.

SOHO, LONDON   OCTOBER 25, 2002

Love Came to Visit Me

Love came to visit me,
Shy as a fawn,
But finding me busy, she
Fled with the dawn.

At twenty, the torch of
Resentment was lit,
My rage at injustice
Waxed hot as the pit,
The flux of its lava
Cleared all in its path,
Comrades and enemies
Fled from its wrath.
Yet lovers grew wary
Once novelty waned —
To lie with a panther
Is terror unfeigned.

At thirty, my powers
Seemed mighty to me,
The fruits of my rivals
I shook from the tree,
By guile and by bluster,
By night and by day,
I battered and scattered
The fools from my way;
And women grew willing
To sham and to bluff —
Their trinkets and baubles
Cost little enough.

From forty to fifty,
I sought the abyss,
Each concubines' laughter
As false as her kiss.
We feasted and revelled
And rutted in muck,
Forgetting our peril,
Forgetting to duck,
Forgetting time's arrows
Are sharper than knives,
Grown sick of our swagger —
And sick of our lives.

Then came a miracle.
Loving but stern,
A Muse I knew naught of
Chided me: 'Turn!
Thy towers are faithless
And built upon sand,'
Then haltered and helpless
And led by the hand
I wandered in byways
Of shadow and light,
And seeing no help for it,
Sat down to write.

Love came to visit me,
Shy as a fawn,
But finding me busy, she
Fled with the dawn.

MANDALAY, MUSTIQUE   MARCH 30, 2002

Adieu!

Chance makes brothers but hearts make friends,
Here then, before our friendship ends
As now it must, my friend, be glad
For what we shared — for what we had.

How late we learned, how little we knew
Of those who stood, blade-straight, steel-true
To brace when push had come to shove:
Chance makes brothers — but hearts make love!

CANDLEWOOD LAKE, CONNECTICUT
OCTOBER 23, 2012

⚘ A Note on the Poems ⚘

The following is in response to questions I am often asked at poetry readings.

I began writing poetry, unexpectedly, in September 1999 while recovering from a life-threatening illness. I was then in my early fifties — pretty late as these things go. One reviewer has observed that I write 'like a man obsessed': perhaps I am subconsciously attempting to make up for lost time? I attempt to write for at least three hours a day on the basis of Mark Twain's dictum that 'most inspiration comes from the application of the seat of the pants to the seat of the chair', and constantly make notes, having discovered that if a promising line or subject arrives in my head, I must reduce it to writing immediately. Delay is often fatal to its recovery.

For the first four or five years I found myself writing four or even five poems a week — a virtual cataract. This has now settled down to two a week or less.

Sometimes I write poetry directly onto my computer. No difference is apparent (to me at least) in the quality of poems created on my computer compared with those begun on paper. When I'm done with a poem, I squirrel it away and try not to refer to it for a year or two, revising only to make selections for a new book or when preparing for a poetry tour. I keep in mind the observation of an earlier poet who said that no poem is ever really 'finished'; merely 'finished *with*' by its author.

Occasionally, I get stuck. Either I cannot write anything worthwhile or I suspect that the form or meter I am wrestling with has usurped the poem's original *raison d'être*. Should this occur, I force myself to abandon the blighter and bang it in a folder marked 'Poems In Progress'. In the early days I tended to soldier on, which often led to second-rate work. Other writers have helped me to come to understand that structure is merely a vessel, not the wine, and that spoiled wine in a fancy decanter is vinegar by any other name. I have also learned that a bad poem, or one merely strong in the weak places, is still a bad poem, no matter what the cost of its birth pains. Some poems arrive effortlessly, others are the result of months of graft. There appears to be (forgive the pun) no rhyme or reason to it.

Audience reaction plays a part in the selection of poems for a new book. While no single audience is infallible, their sustained, collective view is very nearly so, in my experience. Booze helps, but only for up to an hour or so following the first glass of wine; after that, deeply mortifying gibberish is the usual result. Reading the work of other poets is inspirational, but dangerously beguiling. I love to read poetry, but now separate that activity from my own verse-making.

What of intent? Do I write poetry to be performed, to be recorded, or to sit quietly on the page? As anyone familiar with the subject will confirm, some of our finest poets are, or were, poor readers of their own work. (To test this, visit the wonderful website created by Richard Carrington and Andrew Motion, **www.poetryarchive.org** which features, alongside much else, historical recordings by outstanding poets.) Even so, poetry, in essence, is an oral art, a form of song older by far than prose. Rhyme and meter developed partly as a mnemonic device — long before the first hieroglyphs were scratched on rock or bark.

The answer, then, is that I write poetry to be read aloud while knowing that many readers will not follow suit; knowing, too, that only a small percentage will ever attend one of my readings. Instead, my publishers include a free audio CD with my books. Having heard actors from the Royal Shakespeare Company reading my poetry on stage, I am aware that I have neither the talent nor training to match them. Even so, I sit in a studio three or four times a year recording my work. These recordings appear in the audio CDs found in my books, on my own website and others, on the special audio books created by libraries for the blind and, when I'm lucky, on various radio programmes.

Does it all matter? Years ago, a woman came up to me after a poetry reading. She was crying softly. As I signed her book, she kept saying: 'How could you know? How could you know? You are not a mother. How could you know?' She squeezed my shoulder as her husband led her away into the night. So, yes. It bloody well *does* matter — to me and to her, at least.

While it is idle for authors to feign total indifference to applause or brickbats, all in all, I am convinced that I write mainly for myself. I know I would continue to write verse if no other soul in the world expressed interest. I write to discover who I am, to escape the carapace inherited from a life in commerce, to stave off a predilection for other addictions and, primarily, to experience the sheer joy of weaving words to shape ideas. As a somewhat noisome beast, perhaps I should have inflicted my verse-making onto an unsuspecting world anonymously, using a *nom de plume* — the very advice I received from well-meaning friends — but to have done so would have deprived me of the pleasure of performing my work in public.

As Lord Chesterton remarked: 'It is hell to write but heaven to have written.' Amen to that, would say most writers. Why then do we continue to descend into the depths of Chesterton's hell? For some, like Dr. Johnson, the answer might be, 'to make a living': (not that I believe him for a minute). For others, 'to make a reputation' or simply, 'because I can'. For me, it is the result of a chance discovery made ten years ago in a hospital bed: that the flame of poetry cauterises the wound of life as nothing else can.

Any reader wishing to learn more, or wishing to read more of my poetry (published and unpublished) will find a warm welcome on my website at **www.felixdennis.com**

A Note on the Eric Gill Society
(Ditchling Museum of Art+Craft)

Eric Gill (1882–1940) was one of Britain's most innovative and successful artists of the early 20th century. He started his career in 1904 as a letter cutter, creating a revolutionary approach to this traditional craft. In 1908 he began wood engraving and in 1909 direct carving sculpture in Ditchling, Sussex. In both of these media he overturned traditional approaches and inspired other artists to new ways of working.

Gill also became an accomplished essayist, designer, typographer, illustrator, book designer, printer and architect. His sculptures adorn many important buildings in London and elsewhere, including the BBC and Westminster Cathedral and his typography is still widely used. Both typefaces within the book you are holding were designed by him.

The Eric Gill Society exists to promote the enjoyment, appreciation and understanding of the work of Eric Gill and of the craftworkers and artists associated with him in Ditchling and elsewhere and to support the Ditchling Museum of Art+Craft in achieving the same aim.

ERIC GILL SOCIETY
DITCHLING MUSEUM
OF ART+CRAFT

For more information on
Eric Gill and his associates, go to:
Website: **www.ericgill.org.uk**
Facebook: **Eric Gill Society**
Pinterest: **ericgillsoc**

Eric Gill
Self-Portrait, 1927, Wood engraving

✒ Acknowledgements ✒

For a long while, I thought of this as the book I would never live to finish, let alone see. Although *Love, Of A Kind* is dedicated to Richard Neville (and by extension to fellow London OZ conspirators of the 1960s including, Louise Ferrier, Martin Sharp, Andrew Fisher, Jim Anderson and Marsha Rowe among a host of others) it is also a hymn of thanks to those whose professionalism, kindness and love kept me alive in 2012.

To thank everyone involved in that process is beyond my power, but here is a short list. Let me apologise in advance for numerous omissions: David Bliss, Ian Leggett, Toby Fisher, Igor and Marion Kolodotschko, my brother, Julian, and Marie-France Demolis walked me through the valley of the shadow of death. Doctors, surgeons, consultants, heads of hospital departments, nurses *et* al include the following — I trust that they will forgive the lack of professional titles and credentials so as to avoid repetition: Kamran Ahmed, Dawn Adamson, Chris Alcock, Jenny Black, Michael Bunbury, Dawn Carnell, Neil Cohen, Graham Cox, Alan Doherty, Kris Dowdeswell, Kumni Fasanmade, Gemma Graham, Carol Harris, Iain Hutchison, Julie Howard, Nicholas Kalavrezos, Lee Kames, Vanessa Linton, Milton Maltz, Simon Morley, Jeni Norris, Sandip Popat, Jacky Rawlings, Robin Russell, Tim Shackley, Amen Sibtain, Clare Spencer, Michael Stelakis, Rebecca Turner, Julia Varga and Wai Wong. Of these, Michael Bunbury, Milton Maltz, Tim Shackley, Julie Howard, Chris Alcock and surgeon Graham Cox bore the brunt of responsibility for my treatment and care and I am very, very grateful to them.

I am one of those who 'live more lives than one' (see page 65). As such, the temptation is to use the opportunity of an acknowledgements page like this to publicly thank those who work with me in other lives: for example in planning a broadleaf forest and planting tens of thousands of trees each year; running six homes around the globe together with a substantial Warwickshire farm and estate; publishing many magazines and launching a growing stable of digital brands; keeping a private office humming and remembering to pay my debts, collect my earnings and audit my accounts. Without competent colleagues, friends and professionals to do all that, I could never find the time to write poetry.

Even so, just for once, I am going to resist temptation and stick to thanking those who helped on *Love, Of A Kind* and 'The Cut-Throat Tour 2013' which will support it. Caroline Rush was responsible for producing both the book and the tour. Don Atyeo, Moni Mannings, Deborah Boehm, Simon Rae and Suzen Murakoshi, early 'readers' of the poems, suggested many cuts and inclusions. Beckie Jezzard designed my book and selected the illustrations by that old reprobate, Eric Gill. Fiona MacIntyre and Carey Smith of Ebury Press published it. George Taylor wrote the music for the CD and organised the studio voice recordings. Nicky Baker arranged for the CD to be made. Bill Sanderson created the front cover image. Simon Turtle and Lucinda Batchelor took author photographs.

Mick Watson, Thom Stretton and their Class Act colleagues will stage our 30-city 'Cut-Throat Tour 2013' promoting *Love, Of A Kind* in the UK and Europe. Wendy Kasabian and Caroline will mother-hen the tour. Andrew Boyd, Selina Robinson and Lance Welch will count the beans and pay the bills. *The Week* magazine will proudly sponsor the tour (I hope!). Cathy Galt, Toby Fisher, Catherine Law, Michael Hyman and Lloyd Warren will do their best to ensure I arrive at gigs suitably attired and on time. Jerina Hardy and Abi Spooner, are in charge of PR and promo marketing, respectively. Sebastian Rich will be taking tour photographs (in between rushing off to get himself shot at in war zones). Jonathan Noone will work the internet marketing and ticketing arrangements. Sharon Islam will feed me, (when I remember to eat, that is). And through it all, Marie-France will remain the love of my life and the companion of my heart.

Exhausting isn't it? And that is just one of my lives!

Thank you so much to everyone mentioned here — and thank you, too, to the scores of others who work with me and make me one of the luckiest people alive. I do try not to forget that fact each day, but the poet, the performer, the entrepreneur and the planter within me are often in a state of armed truce and occasionally barely on speaking terms one to the other. It is the nature of the beast. Long may it remain so.

Appendix

Ballad of the Goodly Fere

Simon Zelotes speaketh it somewhile after the Crucifixion

HA' we lost the goodliest fere o' all
For the priests and the gallows tree?
Aye lover he was of brawny men,
O' ships and the open sea.

When they came wi' a host to take Our Man
His smile was good to see,
'First let these go!' quo' our Goodly Fere,
'Or I'll see ye damned," says he.

Aye he sent us out through the crossed high spears
And the scorn of his laugh rang free,
'Why took ye not me when I walked about
Alone in the town?' says he.

Oh we drank his 'Hale' in the good red wine
When we last made company.
No capon priest was the Goodly Fere,
But a man o' men was he.

I ha' seen him drive a hundred men
Wi' a bundle o' cords swung free,
That they took the high and holy house
For their pawn and treasury.

They'll no' get him a' in a book, I think,
Though they write it cunningly;
No mouse of the scrolls was the Goodly Fere
But aye loved the open sea.

If they think they ha' snared our Goodly Fere
They are fools to the last degree.
'I'll go to the feast,' quo' our Goodly Fere,
'Though I go to the gallows tree.'

'Ye ha' seen me heal the lame and blind,
And wake the dead,' says he.
'Ye shall see one thing to master all:
'Tis how a brave man dies on the tree.'

A son of God was the Goodly Fere
That bade us his brothers be.
I ha' seen him cow a thousand men.
I have seen him upon the tree.

He cried no cry when they drave the nails
And the blood gushed hot and free.
The hounds of the crimson sky gave tongue,
But never a cry cried he.

I ha' seen him cow a thousand men
On the hills o' Galilee.
They whined as he walked out calm between,
Wi' his eyes like the gray o' the sea.

Like the sea that brooks no voyaging,
With the winds unleashed and free,
Like the sea that he cowed at Genseret
Wi' twey words spoke suddenly.

A master of men was the Goodly Fere,
A mate of the wind and sea.
If they think they ha' slain our Goodly Fere
They are fools eternally.

I ha' seen him eat o' the honey-comb
Sin' they nailed him to the tree.

BY EZRA POUND
(First published in 1909)

~ Index ~

🌿 Felix Dennis 🌿

Felix Dennis is one of Britain's best-loved poets. His six previous books of poetry are all still in print. His poetry has been performed by The Royal Shakespeare Company on both sides of the Atlantic and has enjoyed wide success on the radio, in scores of English language newspapers and on countless internet sites.

Sky Arts recently aired an hour-long television documentary focused on his poetry and organisations as diverse as The Royal Marines and The National Trust have adopted his poems for their own use. His hugely popular poetry recitals pack theatres across Britain, Ireland and the USA.

As a lover of trees, his lifetime ambition is the planting of a large native forest in the Heart of England. He has homes in England, the USA and St. Vincent and the Grenadines.

For more of his poetry or to watch him performing live visit **www.felixdennis.com**

To view progress on Felix's forest project visit **www.heartofenglandforest.com**

'Weeping may endure for a night,
but joy cometh in the morning.'

— *Psalms 30:5*